MW00608812

WASHBURN UNIVERSITY
150 Years

By Monroe Dodd

Foreword by Bob Dole

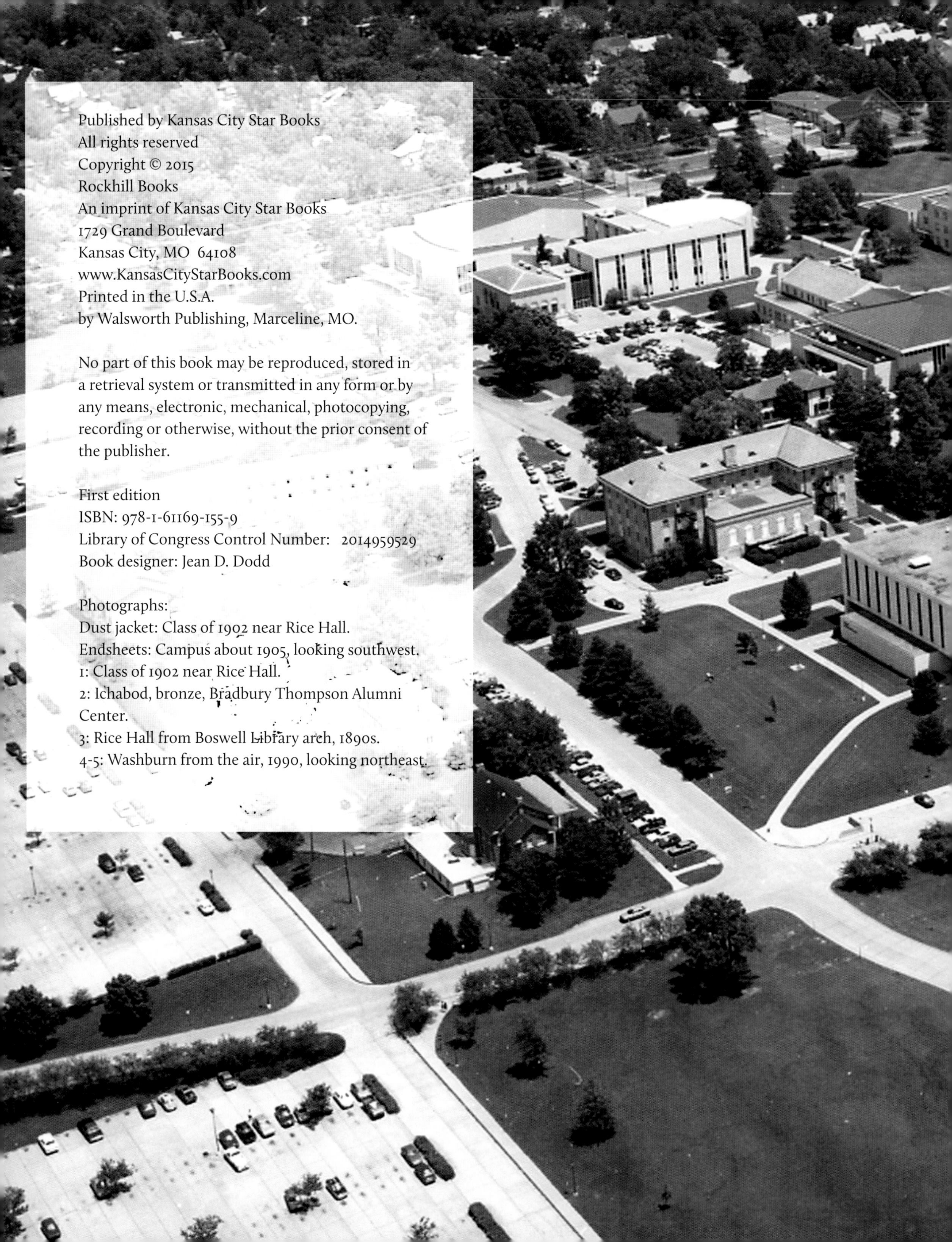

Published by Kansas City Star Books

Rockhill Books
An imprint of Kansas City Star Books
1729 Grand Boulevard
Kansas City, MO 64108
www.KansasCityStarBooks.com
Printed in the U.S.A.
by Walsworth Publishing, Marceline, MO.

First edition
ISBN: 978-1-61169-155-9
Library of Congress Control Number: 2014959529
Book designer: Jean D. Dodd

Photographs:
Dust jacket: Class of 1902 near Rice Hall.
Endsheets: Campus about 1905, looking southwest.
1: Class of 1902 near Rice Hall.
2: Ichabod, bronze, Bradbury Thompson Alumni Center.
3: Rice Hall from Boswell Library arch, 1890s.
4-5: Washburn from the air, 1990, looking northeast.

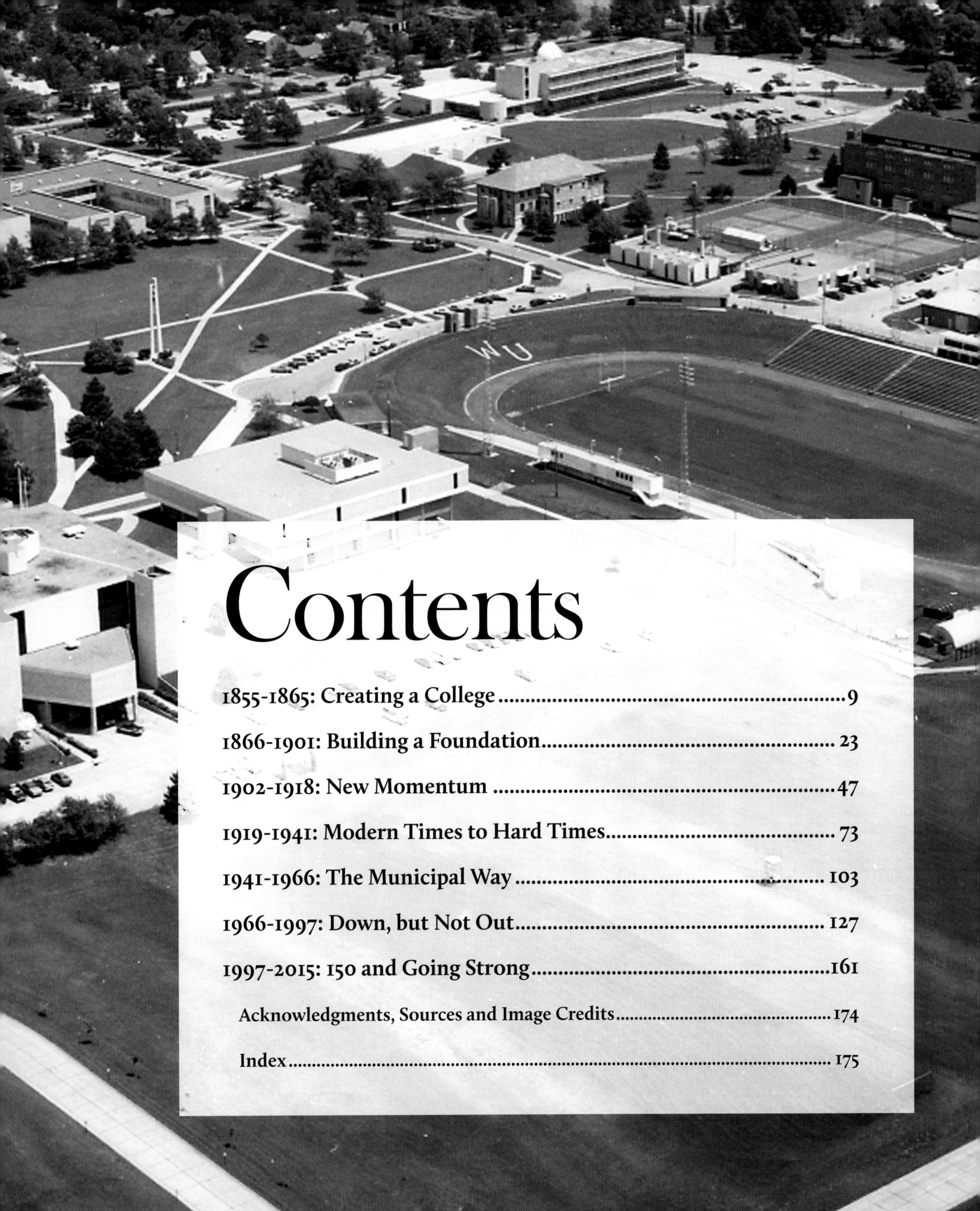

Contents

MULVANE PERMIT PARKING ONLY
MULVANE PERMIT PARKING ONLY
MULVANE PERMIT PARKING ONLY
CENTER

Foreword

Washburn sprang from the minds of some of American history's most devout and determined pioneers, who made the grueling journey west both to create a new home for themselves and to change the course of history. First they fought to turn back the forces of slavery — and succeeded. Then they strove to create a moral and educated people. Washburn was the result.

With few funds and sometimes with their own labor, the founders built a college. Facing never-ending shortages of money, they persevered and created an institution that has not only endured but also expanded and excelled over a century and a half.

Bob Dole

At 150, Washburn bears little physical resemblance to its earliest incarnation. A tornado that smashed through the campus in 1966 made sure of that. Yet just as its founders met Washburn's earliest challenges, the administrators, faculty, students and friends of Washburn rose to rebuild it from the storm's destruction.

Today, Washburn continues to adapt dynamically to the needs of its community and of Kansas, recognizing their growing diversity and also adapting to changes in technology while keeping its tradition as a teaching institution.

If I've had any success throughout my life, I primarily credit that success to my years at Washburn. My professors taught me discipline and the necessity of hard work. In addition to the outstanding academic instruction on campus, I also enjoyed having the opportunity to interact with students from across the country. As I look back over the years, graduation from Washburn was a high point in my life. My Washburn degrees have served me well — providing me with solid opportunities following my injuries during World War II. For my generation, which had won a war but had to work hard to gain the education that would bring a better future, Washburn gave us a home and a new start.

Today I hardly recognize the Washburn campus because of its tremendous growth and change over the years, but it remains a place I will always call "home."

SENATOR BOB DOLE
Washburn B.A., J.D., 1952
Member, U.S. House of Representatives, 1961-1969
U.S. Senate, 1969-1996

Facing page: Washburn's Living Learning Center.

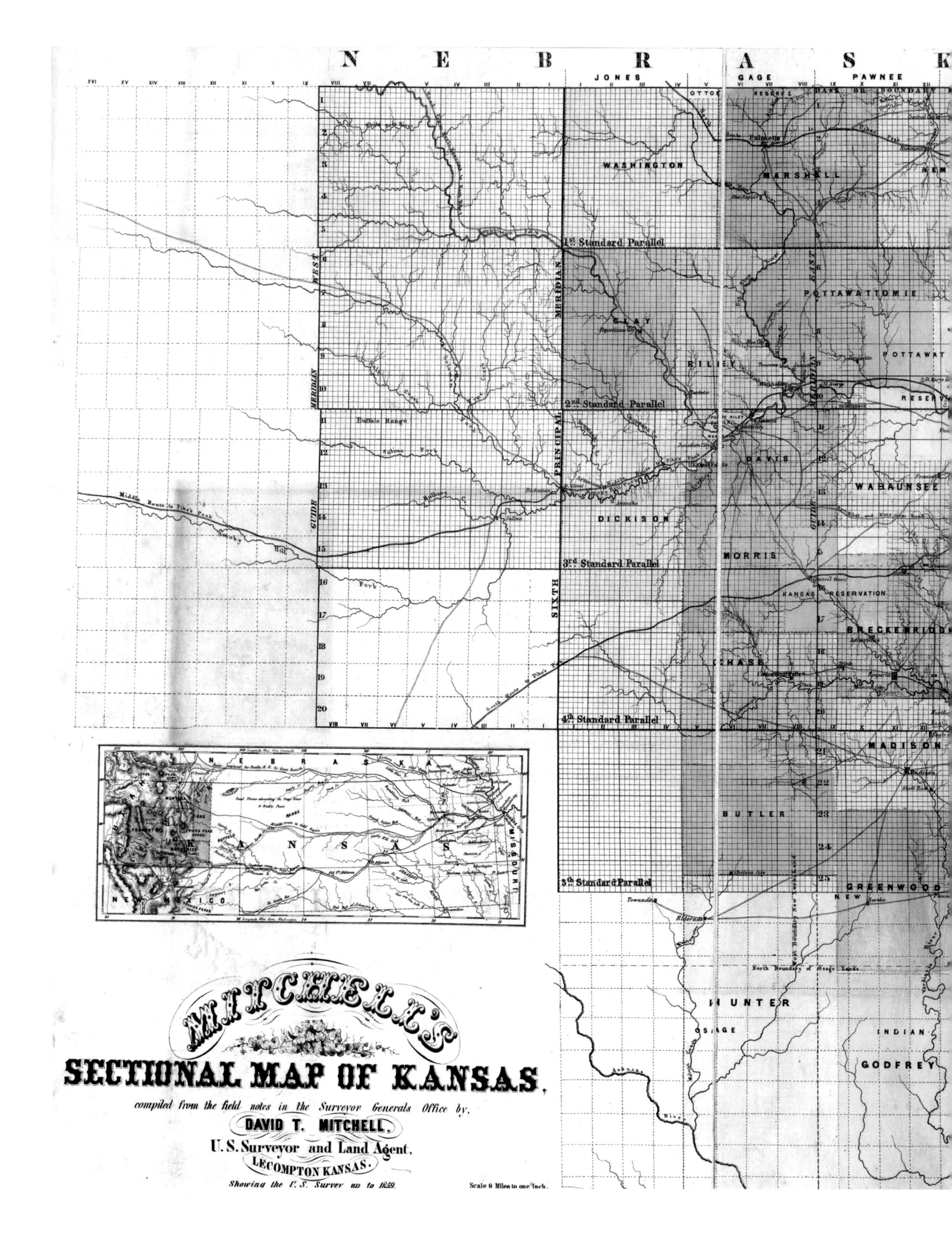
NEBRASKA
WASHINGTON
MARSHALL
POTTAWATTOMIE
CLAY
RILEY
DAVIS
WABAUNSEE
DICKISON
MORRIS
KANSAS RESERVATION
BRECKENRIDGE
CHASE
MADISON
BUTLER
GREENWOOD
HUNTER
OSAGE
INDIAN
GODFREY
1st. Standard Parallel
2nd. Standard Parallel
3rd. Standard Parallel
4th. Standard Parallel
5th. Standard Parallel
PRINCIPAL
SIXTH
MERIDIAN
GUIDE
WEST
EAST
Middle Route to Pike's Peak
South Route to Pike's Peak
Buffalo Range
North Boundary of Osage Lands
West Boundary New York Land
MITCHELL'S
SECTIONAL MAP OF KANSAS,
compiled from the field notes in the Surveyor Generals Office by,
DAVID T. MITCHELL,
U.S. Surveyor and Land Agent,
LECOMPTON KANSAS.
Showing the U.S. Survey up to 1859.
Scale 9 Miles to one Inch.

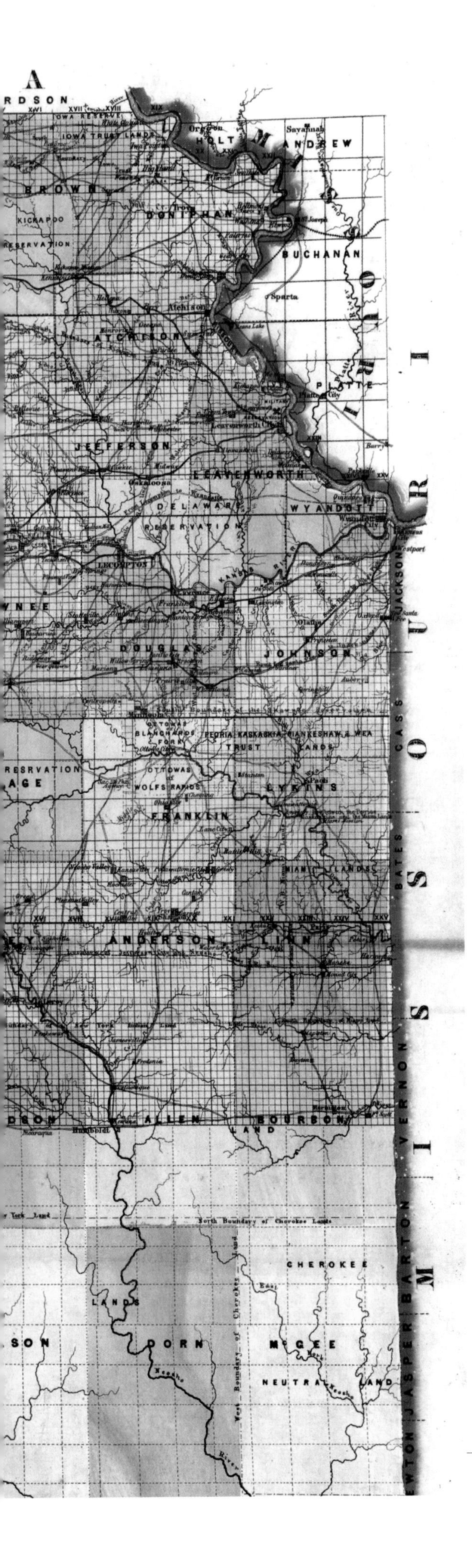

1855-1865

Creating a College

Washburn began as an idea.

The idea sprang from the convictions of New Englanders whose ancestors had followed the strict and spare tenets of Puritanism. In the 1850s, stirred to action by the political storm over slavery in the United States, these New Englanders focused on the territory where the debate was hottest — the frontier of Kansas. They dedicated themselves to bringing to that frontier liberty, learning and the Lord.

Some of them backed their fervor with money, of which there was plenty in old New England from shipping, manufacturing and finance. A few went farther. They made the difficult trek west by rail, river, road and trail — nearly 1,500 miles, all the way to the Missouri River and past it to the new Kansas Territory.

On bare prairie, they built cabins, organized themselves and dreamed up towns. In some places the New Englanders were outnumbered, yet their education, confidence and strong beliefs propelled them to leadership. They would build Kansas in their own image, establish churches — Puritans by then called themselves Congregationalists — and start schools.

"It shall be our aim," said a statement adopted by a group of Congregationalists meeting in the new village of Topeka, "to transplant the principles and institutions of the Puritans to these fertile plains."

To Congregationalists, the best ministers were learned ones, and the best citizenry was also educated. It wasn't long before some of them began planning a college in Kansas Territory.

Kansas Territory, 1859.

Numbers

Population, 1860

- Kansas: 107,206
- Topeka: 759

Accomplishing that would require determination. In the first years after the opening of the territory, the middle 1850s, the odds figured against them. Common sense might have argued that they give up. Yet these settlers were fired by a spirit of moral rightness — even moral superiority. They proved tough, and equal to the task.

From them came Washburn, the idea and the fact.

"It shall be our aim to transplant the principles and institutions of the Puritans to these fertile plains."

– From a statement adopted by a group of Congregationalists meeting in the new village of Topeka.

True believers

Scholars have estimated that fewer than 250,000 Americans in the 1850s were Congregationalists. As the name implies, Congregational churches maintained considerable independence from one another and from any central governance. They were united, however, in passionate opposition to slavery.

The Kansas-Nebraska Act of 1854 turned fervor into anti-slavery fever. For three and a half decades, the Missouri Compromise had prohibited slavery in American territories — and thus future states — north of a line running west from Missouri's southern border. Like all compromises, this one did not thoroughly please everyone, but it supposedly fixed permanently the territories where everyone would remain free. Suddenly, that compromise was erased by the Kansas-Nebraska Act, which allowed the people of any new territory, north or south of the line, to determine whether the future state would be slave or free. Few Americans complained more strongly or were more determined to fight slavery in the new land than the Congregationalists from New England.

In spring 1855, a determined Congregationalist named John Ritchey settled near the nascent community of Topeka, founded only months earlier and consisting of a few log or sod houses scattered beside the Kansas River.

Ritchey was neither particularly young — 37 years old that year — nor was he from New England. He was born in Ohio and while a boy moved with his family to Indiana. Still, the same abolitionist spirit burned in him that burned in his New England brethren. In everything — from hatred of slavery to women's suffrage to temperance — Ritchey lived, thought and argued with vigor. He had come to Kansas to create a new world.

Ritchey and his wife built a crude home of sod on the windy prairie south of the Topeka settlement. It had one room with a bare floor and nail kegs for chairs.

The land where the Ritcheys settled proved harsh and demanding. Mary Jane Ritchey, John Ritchey's wife, recalled awakening several times in the winter of 1855-1856 and finding snow on the blankets. On Christmas Day 1855, the settlers reported that the temperature plunged to 17 degrees below zero.

Besides heat, cold, wind and storm, settlers also faced pro-slavers, who dominated some nearby Kansas towns and also the territorial government. In the middle and late 1850s, the national government, which ran the territory, was sympathetic to slavery.

One hopeful young minister on his way to Kansas from Connecticut, Lewis Bodwell, found just how difficult those pro-slavery forces could be. Headed west in September 1856, Bodwell learned that pro-slavers were prohibiting northern immigrants from crossing the Missouri River into Kansas Territory. Attempting to enter through Nebraska with a wagon train of fellow northerners, he and others were arrested by federal troops who found muskets and sabers in some of the wagons. Bodwell was freed only after the

One intrepid man, looking to redeem mankind

"Radical of Radicals," *The Leavenworth Times* said of John Ritchey, "the extremist on all points, par excellence."

He arrived in Topeka in April 1855, and within a year was accepted into the Town Company, the men who founded the tiny settlement near the Kansas River.

He could be good-humored and likable, yet quick to state his views to anyone who would listen. Many of those views were extreme for the time. *The Times* described him as "ultra abolitionist, woman's rights man, teetotaler...looking eagerly and earnestly for the ultimate redemption of mankind from all oppressions, abuses and vices."

John and Mary Jane Ritchie, first spelled "Ritchey."

Among his early friends was another outspoken anti-slavery man, John Brown, whom Ritchey met in Lawrence. Ritchey's home in Topeka sheltered slaves escaping by way of the Underground Railroad. In later years, he would give land to African-Americans for homes near Topeka and for plots in a cemetery.

Before moving to Kansas, Ritchey had done well buying and selling land in Indiana, a skill he translated to Kansas. Only five months before his arrival, nine investors had formed the Town Association of Topeka, and Ritchey joined that group. The association was formed to divvy up land and resell it to prospective residents and business owners.

He was one of the organizers of the first Congregational Church, and also had an interest in higher education, spurred by a visit to Knox College in Galesburg, Illinois — reportedly made on his trip west to settle in Kansas. Not surprisingly, as early as 1856 he talked up the idea of a college. That same year Ritchey, as a member of the free-state militia, reportedly took part in raids on several Kansas towns known to be dominated by pro-slavery partisans, or by neutral folks. Pro-slavers had blocked wagons bringing supplies to anti-slavery Topeka, and the raids were aimed at re-supplying the town.

Federal troops from Forts Leavenworth and Riley arrested about one hundred of the anti-slavery raiders and jailed them in Lecompton. Ritchey was one. With some of the others, he escaped in late 1856 and returned briefly to Indiana. By 1857 he was back in Topeka, believing that the territorial governor had granted amnesty to him and other raiders. The federal courts, however, were not under the governor's control.

In late April 1860, a deputy U.S. marshal named Leonard Arms tried to arrest Ritchey on the old federal charge, went to Ritchey's home, defied warnings to leave, and was shot to death. Amid an aroused and pro-Ritchey citizenry, a local judge pronounced the deed " justifiable in the sight of God and man." Ritchey went free.

He remained free with his opinions. So strident were his complaints about a fellow Congregationalist — evidently made because Ritchey simply did not like the man — that the Congregational church excommunicated him. Nevertheless, his own congregation allowed him to continue attending.

When the Civil War began in April 1861, Ritchey volunteered for the Union Army, changing the way he spelled his name to Ritchie. Family legend said he wanted to differentiate himself from some other person named Ritchey. He rose to colonel, recruiting a regiment from Indian reservations in eastern Kansas and the Indian Territory to the south. His fellow officers complained about "excessive zeal" on his part, not surprising given that Ritchie had a habit of "seizing hold of staff officers" when he disagreed with them.

After the war, Ritchie continued to make plain his views. In 1867, he gave the welcoming speech for Susan B. Anthony when she visited Topeka.

John Ritchie died in 1887. A plaque mounted on a stone at the south side of Benton Hall bears his name.

group reached an agreement with the territorial governor at Topeka.

Bodwell learned quickly about life in the territory. A year later, another Congregational minister saw Bodwell at a free-state meeting, wearing a blanket over his shoulders.

"Under the blanket were plainly visible the muzzle of a Sharps rife and the hilt of a Colt's revolver," the minister recalled of Bodwell. "His carbine and revolver were not carried altogether as ornaments; for the firm setting of his lips and the flashing of his keen black eye plainly showed that when he once felt in duty called upon to shoot, it would be very unpleasant for somebody."

In 1856 "Ruffians," a name attached to pro-slavery forces by the free-soil backers, blocked roads or otherwise threatened deliveries to Topeka of food and other goods from Leavenworth or Westport. Topekans and other free-staters, mustering themselves into companies of militia, raided pro-slavery towns such as Ozawkie and Tecumseh and took by force the items they needed or wanted.

Eventually, events in Kansas swung the way of the free-state movement. As sentiment gained among Kansas settlers to ban slavery in their future state, New England-style civilization secured a foothold. The college idea gained traction. Indeed, according to longtime Washburn history professor Bill Wagnon, the idea was a key to the town builders' vision for a growing community.

"Right away they identified the things the needed for success," Wagnon says, "and a college was one of those."

Grand ideas

As early as April 1856, John Ritchey entertained fellow Congregationalists on his property outside Topeka. One visitor, Harrison Hannahs, recalled years later that, although "one of the Kansas zephyrs was blowing about 60 miles an hour," he and Ritchey "waded against the current" out to a slight rise on the prairie. Ritchey believed the property, part of a quarter-section of land owned by a man named George Davis, would make an ideal campus for a college.

In early 1857, as northern and anti-slavery emigrants poured into Kansas, a group of Congregationalists formed a General Association of Congregational Ministers and Churches in Kansas, which resolved to proceed with planning for an institution to create educated ministers and educated congregations.

On April 25, the association named a committee of five members from various commu-

Lewis Bodwell

Lewis Bodwell was born in Connecticut, taught in New Jersey, and became a minister in New York. In summer 1856, he made friends with several students at Andover Theological Seminary in Massachusetts who were deeply interested in the battle over slavery in Kansas Territory. They called themselves the Kansas Missionary Band. With backing from the American Home Missionary Society of New York, Bodwell left for Kansas in September 1856.

After various trials getting past federal authorities, he arrived in Topeka and began calling on the members of the tiny church, sleeping each night wherever he could find a spot on the prairie. He preached his first sermon October 26, at Constitution Hall, the only meeting room available, and soon began preaching at other churches. A strong opponent of alcohol, he joined Congregationalists and members of other denominations in opposing saloons. Like his nities to search for a site. Among its number were Ritchey, who had already helped found a Congregational church in Topeka, and Bodwell, who had become its pastor. The committee also included representatives from Lawrence and other nearby towns. In early October 1858, the committee made its report to the General Association: The preferred site would be a 160-acre tract "within a mile and a half of Topeka" — the very place Ritchey, chairman of the committee, had shown to Harrison Hannahs.

Free Congregational Church, Topeka, early 1860s.

The panel also proposed to acquire land inside the townsite and additional larger acreage outside it to form an endowment. A college, the committee said, would be ready to commence within 13 months — by January 1, 1860. The General Association approved, named a Board of Trustees to oversee the institution and placed Bodwell at its head. Then, evidently in an attempt to make the Topekans show they were serious, the association allowed the effort only three months.

Ritchey and others hurried to make deals. They reported success in acquiring 820 acres in Shawnee County for an endowment and 20 acres inside the limits of Topeka. However, Davis, who owned the 160 acres that formed the centerpiece of the effort — Ritchey's favored college site — set terms that Ritchey found impossible to meet.

Then word reached Topeka about the Colorado gold strikes of 1858. George Davis could not resist the temptation to go make his fortune, so he relented and in early 1859 offered the land to Ritchey and the Congregationalists for cash. This they did not have — Topeka boasted not a single bank at the time

co-religionists of the day, Bodwell also frowned on dancing, theater-going, use of tobacco and violating the Sabbath by working or participating in entertainments.

Through the territorial years and Civil War, Bodwell constantly carried a rifle or a revolver in case a fight broke out. As a pastor, however, Bodwell was reported to have had a friendly and helpful nature, and he was well respected. In April 1857, at a meeting of Congregationalist ministers, he was named to the committee to consider the building of a college. When Topeka's first attempt could not meet the church leaders' terms, Bodwell declared the bid a failure and the church turned to a bid from Lawrence. Bodwell's actions cost him friends in his own town. By 1860, he was ready to quit and become a traveling agent of the American Home Missionary Society.

After the Civil War, Bodwell returned as pastor of the Congregational Church, which had changed its name with the demise of slavery from "Free" to "First" Congregational. In 1869, because of his wife's ill health, Bodwell resigned and moved her to a hospital in Clifton Springs, New York, where he died in 1894.

1854-1865

1854: On May 30, the Kansas-Nebraska Act created the Kansas Territory and allowed settlers of it and other territories in the American West to decide whether they would be slave or free – On December 5, nine men formed the Topeka Town Association.

1855: A Congregational church was organized in Topeka.

1857: Kansas Congregationalists named a committee to find a site for a college.

1858: Kansas Congregationalists accepted a college proposal by Topekans.

1859: A 160-acre tract south of Topeka was acquired for a college through the efforts of Harvey Rice and John Ritchey.
1860: After offering Lawrence a chance for the college, which it could not fulfill, Congregationalists turned back to Topeka.
1861: Kansas admitted as a free state. Civil War began. Progress on college delayed.
1865: On February 6, a Shawnee County judge approved articles of incorporation drafted by a Board of Trustees to create Lincoln College.

The Topeka of the college founders: Kansas Avenue in the early 1860s.

— but they thought they could get it from old friends in New England. Ritchey offered to mortgage his own farmstead, a separate 160-acre tract, to anyone who would lend money. With that promise in hand, one of the trustees and a friend of Ritchey's, Harvey D. Rice, headed for New England, planning to get a loan using Ritchey's farm as collateral.

Rice, having lived a decade in Hartford, Connecticut, was acquainted with prominent residents there, and readily raised about $900. But George Davis wanted more than that, and securing more proved difficult. As Rice recalled years later, he had become discouraged until one April afternoon he got an invitation to the home of Henry Ward Beecher's half-sister, Isabella Beecher Hooker, and her husband, John Hooker, a descendant of the man who founded Hartford.

At their home that day, Rice found an intellectually formidable group of women, among them Harriett Beecher Stowe, author of the abolitionist novel *Uncle Tom's Cabin*. Isabella Beecher Hooker herself would become a leader of the American suffragist movement. Now, the women's primary concern was ending slavery.

Upon arriving home, Harvey Rice received a rude shock. Without waiting for his return, the Congregationalists' General Association already had declared the Topeka effort a failure....

As a representative from the western battleground of Kansas Territory, Rice proved interesting to them, and his entreaties fell on receptive ears. The women spoke with their husbands, and lawyer John Hooker was persuaded, with his partner, to lend the college effort $1,100. With $2,000 in hand and Ritchey's farm as his lenders' collateral, Rice headed back to Kansas.

A setback

Upon arriving home, Harvey Rice received a rude shock. Without waiting for his return, the Congregationalists' General Association already had declared the Topeka effort a failure and asked for new college proposals from other towns. Dismayed but not defeated, Rice turned over the loan proceeds to Ritchey, who negotiated a deal for the Davis farm for $1,600. Ritchey took over the deed for the 160 acres, and he and Rice awaited further developments.

Lawrence, then a larger city than Topeka, entered an impressive-sounding bid. Congregationalists and other residents promised land and money for an institution to serve as a monument to the struggle against slavery. It would be named "Monumental College." However, a downturn in the economy aggravated by drought caused thousands of settlers to leave Kansas Territory, and the promises of the Lawrence college promoters proved to be far handsomer than the results. By May 1860, the Lawrence backers admitted that they could not fulfill their pledge.

The General Association turned again to Topeka. The next year, 1861, when Kansas had achieved statehood, the association asked for a deed to the 160 acres as a future home for a school that tentatively would be called the Topeka Institute. Rice and Ritchey's wife drew up the deed. John Ritchey was away, having joined the Union Army as the Civil War began — and spelling his name "Ritchie" when he did so. The Hartford group that had lent the $1,100 through Harvey Rice in return for Ritchie's mortgage on his home property discharged the mortgage on December 13, 1861. They acknowledged receiving "full payment," presumably from Ritchie.

There, matters ground to a halt. The combination of the Civil War, a lingering drought

Bird's eye view of Topeka, created in 1869, accurately placed Washburn College at its first site, 10th and Jackson streets, but exaggerated progress on the Kansas Capitol, which would require decades to complete.

and a general business decline would stifle the Topeka Congregationalists' college effort for four more years.

The war also stifled the spread of Congregationalism in Kansas. Lewis Bodwell, who had quit as pastor in Topeka and become an agent of the American Home Missionary Society, lamented to his supervisors that at least 17 Kansas counties had no one to preach a "pure & intelligently taught gospel." Kansas had plenty of another kind of preaching, Bodwell continued, more emotional and less cerebral — "little better than heathenism slightly civilized."

"Honesty, truthfulness, peacefulness, study of the word & regard for the Sabbath," he said, "seldom long surviving the two or three weeks of a ... season of shouting, screaming, dancing and rolling on the floor; called a revival!"

To Bodwell and his co-religionists, the answer to this religious fanaticism remained clear: Create a college in the proper mold — namely, the Congregational mold — and educate ministers of the future.

Harrison Hannahs, a trustee with Ritchie, Rice and others.

"Situated near the heart of the continent, it will stand sentinel evermore over the broad land whose union he consummated."

— Lincoln College publication, referring to the assassinated president.

In honor — and in memoriam

By early 1865, when Union prospects for victory seemed assured, the General Association in Kansas agreed that it was time to move forward with the college. On January 25, the men who would incorporate the institution, Congregationalist ministers and laymen all, assembled in Topeka. Three of the nine "incorporators" — Harvey Rice, Lewis Bodwell and Harrison Hannahs — also had served with the original trustees named in 1858. Now, they drew up Articles of Association with a section that, among other things promised to "afford to all classes, without distinction of color, the advantages of a liberal education."

They also produced a new name to replace "Topeka Institute." It would be called Lincoln College, after the president who had led the country through the Civil War and who had emancipated slaves in the South.

According to state law, the paperwork was submitted to a Shawnee County probate judge and an appraisal was made of the available property and assets, including the 160-acre parcel intended as the site. The total value was set at $7,228. Quickly, Judge Albert I. Winans found everything in order and signed and sealed the documents.

On that day, February 6, 1865, Lincoln College came into existence.

A 13-member Board of Trustees was elected. It included Harvey Rice, John Ritchie, and Harrison Hannahs. As chair, the members chose Peter McVicar, who had replaced Bodwell as pastor of the Congregational Church in Topeka.

On March 27, land records show, Ritchie and his wife received $2,600 from the Lincoln College Board of Trustees for the 160 acres plus two lots on 10th Avenue in Topeka. Because Ritchie had twice deeded the property to the college and the original mortgage on his own farm had been discharged, the transaction possibly was to compensate him. Another interpretation was that it established the value of a donation of the land.

Samuel D. Bowker, a 30-year-old native of Maine and a Congregational minister, was made financial agent of Lincoln College, which meant he would start gathering funds for its operation and endowment. Bowker headed east, where the money was.

Passing through Washington in early March 1865, Bowker called on President Abraham Lincoln. The visit came the week of Lincoln's second inauguration. Lincoln, Bowker later wrote, gave his blessing to the namesake college, "expressed to me his cordial approval of its design and gave assurance of his prospective aid in its behalf."

One month later, Lincoln lay dead from an assassin's bullet. The new college in Kansas promptly dedicated itself to his memory as a monument to "the triumph of freedom over slavery." The trustees saw every reason to do so, citing the facts that Lincoln's rise to national status occurred amid the Kansas troubles over slavery, that Kansas gave him a larger proportion of votes than any other state and that his name was linked strongly to the Union and to free institutions.

A Lincoln College publicity publication waxed eloquent: "Situated near the heart of the continent, it will stand sentinel evermore over the broad land whose union he consummated."

Down to business

As Bowker made his way through the Northeast, he raised several thousand dollars and also acquired books for the future library of the college. But Lincoln College would need home-grown support, too. Contributions from Kansas would demonstrate to donors elsewhere that Kansans were earnest in wanting a college. The education committee of the General Association set a $10,000

Lincoln College building from the northwest, 1867. Construction materials, sheds and tools were for construction of the east wing of the state Capitol.

Article II.

To make said College an engine for the furtherance of those ideas of Civil and religious liberty which actuated our Fathers in the Revolutionary struggle, and which are now achieving a signal victory in the triumph of free principles.

Article III.

To afford to all classes, without distinction of Color, the advantages of a liberal education, thus fitting them for positions of responsibility and usefulness—

Article IV.

To aid deserving young men to obtain an education, such as shall fit them for the gospel ministry, thereby helping to supply the pressing demand for laborers in the States and Territories west of the Missouri River.

Articles of Asso
in the Incorporation of
Lincoln College

We, the Undersigned, desirous of becoming a body corporate and politic, by the name and title of "Trustees of Lincoln College", do associate ourselves together, for the pur-poses set forth in the Preamble and Ar-ticles of Association, adopted by us, at a meeting held in the City of Topek on the 25th day of January 1865, and which read as follows—

Preamble

Desiring to promote the diffusion of knowledge and the advancement of virtue and religion, we do associate ourselves together for the objects and purposes

Getting excited about preserving free institutions

Harvey Rice was in his 30s and an established nurseryman when he attended a gathering in Hartford, Connecticut, of New Englanders troubled by the Kansas-Nebraska Act. It was 1856, and already abolitionists were bringing stories back to the East of pro-slavery outrages in Kansas Territory.

This night, the speaker condemned the laws established by the pro-slavery territorial legislature and described to an appalled audience his capture by border ruffians in the territory. Inspired by the speech, a New Haven man formed a group of men to go to Kansas. Rice joined up.

On the eve of their departure for the West, March 20, 1856, Henry Ward Beecher spoke to the group in a chapel near Yale in New Haven. He rejected the advice given by some northern clergymen to remain calm. Instead, he told the youths, it was perfectly justifiable to get excited about something sufficiently important — and nothing was more important "than to preserve the free institutions of our country." Beecher and a Yale professor raised enough money to supply a rifle along with a Bible for each emigrant to the West. That was the birth of the Beecher Bible Rifle Company, of which Harvey Rice was a part.

Thus inspired, the group arrived in Kansas City, Missouri, at the end of March. They headed west and on April 5 arrived in Topeka, which Rice recalled being "a very sorrowful-looking town." Constitution Hall, a two-story stone structure, was up, along with a crudely built boarding house and hotel. The few houses were log and sod cabins with the earth as floor.

"Indians, buffalos and border ruffians were very numerous, and the latter very troublesome."

— Harvey Rice

"Indians, buffalos and border ruffians were very numerous," Rice said, "and the latter very troublesome."

The group he accompanied traveled on west to Wabaunsee County, but Rice soon returned to Topeka. In early June he made his way back to Connecticut, packed up his family and on September 1 again departed for the West, this time with his family in tow. The trip took until October 22.

After settling in Topeka for good, he added his efforts to founding the college, which included a trip back east to raise funds for the site and eventually building the first structure used for classes at 10th and Jackson.

Rice sat on the Washburn Board of Trustees until his death in 1903. One year earlier, he had appeared at the ceremony naming the college's first permanent building Rice Hall.

goal for Kansas contributions, and hoped to inspire three times as much from donors in the East.

To sustain the college would require an endowment, a sum of money big enough to yield substantial regular returns. From these returns and from tuition would come money to pay teachers, to build, equip and maintain classrooms and offices and to fund other expenses.

The backers of Lincoln College aimed high, telling potential donors that their institution in Kansas would be like Harvard, Dartmouth and Yale, a center of "vigor, manhood, intelligence and truth."

In his efforts in the East, Bowker succeeded in gathering several thousand dollars in pledges. However, the college was soon to learn that some donors would not fulfill their promises. Once Bowker's travel expenses were reimbursed, his trip netted about $2,300. The trustees summoned him back to Kansas to seek contributions closer to home. By December 1865, he was visiting Missouri River towns such as Atchison, Leavenworth and Wyandotte, asking for money. The amount he raised in Kansas neared $10,000 but much of that was payable only over several years and $2,600 of it was not secured by any property.

As a result, Lincoln College began its operations on a shoestring. Undaunted, the trustees marched ahead. Several of them busied themselves with building a structure on what would be a temporary site near downtown. It stood on lots donated by John Ritchie at the northeast corner of 10th and Jackson streets, across from the grounds where the state Capitol would be erected.

The 10th and Jackson structure would serve the college until construction could commence on the 160 acres purchased from George Davis. In 1865, that property was a mile and a half from town and thus considered too remote for potential students.

The trustees commissioned plans for a two-story classroom building at 10th and Jackson, 32 feet by 54 feet, and put the project up for bid. To their surprise, no contractor stepped forward. Several said they doubted that the college could pay them.

Harvey Rice proposed to do the construction himself in return for $7,000. The trustees accepted. Beginning in spring 1865, Rice used his own teams of horses and oxen to haul in lumber and stone. He hired Union soldiers still stationed in Topeka to do labor and did much himself. By late 1865, he was finished — and paid. He produced a limestone-wall building, two stories tall with a meeting hall on the first floor and seven other rooms.

Classes were scheduled to begin in mid-November 1865. Peter McVicar, now president of the trustees, announced that the curriculum would consist of practical courses in addition to liberal arts classes in Greek, Latin and other pursuits. He also announced that Lincoln had acquired a small library, a mineral collection and money from an eastern donor to pay for scholarships. The college issued its first catalog of faculty and courses.

Three faculty members were named for the college-level courses and five for the courses in a preparatory department. The latter program functioned as a high school, a rarity in Kansas in the mid-1860s. It would prepare teenagers for college-level study. Samuel D. Bowker was named principal.

The opening of the school's first term, presumably because of the press of events, was delayed until January 3, 1866. Other troubles had not long stood in the founders' way, and money troubles would not, either.

Decades later, in 1915, the editors of the college yearbook would marvel at the perseverance of the founders, saying:

"It is amazing to think that, in the midst of incessant distractions, when innocent men were being murdered for their opinions, when homes were being destroyed and when Kansas seemed almost a military camp, anyone would be found who would take the time or give the work to establish such a luxury as a college."

To those early and determined founders, a college represented a necessity for a civilized people. They were determined to proceed.

Out-of-towners bound for Lincoln College in Topeka in the late 1860s saw this first: the area surrounding the Kansas Pacific depot.

Samuel D. Bowker, fundraiser and teacher.

1865

Building a Foundation

School days at Lincoln's stone building at 10th and Jackson began precisely at 9 a.m. Students walked through the doors and into the largest room in the structure, the assembly hall. First came 15 minutes of devotional exercises: Bible readings, a hymn and prayer, all led by a member of the faculty. Then came 45-minute class periods — Latin, Greek, English grammar, arithmetic and rhetoric — until 4:15, after which another 15-minute period of devotion ended the school day.

In winter, stoves provided some warmth. In warmer months, open windows provided some cooling.

When Lincoln College opened, three days into the new year of 1866, it had a proud name, a brand-new building, a prominent Board of Trustees, a well-qualified faculty and 38 students, 22 men — one of them African-American — and 16 women.

What Lincoln College did not have was a real college.

In the fifth year of statehood, and the ninth month since the end of the Civil War, Kansas was poor in college-preparatory schools and thus mostly destitute of college-ready youth. Not until 1866 was the first high school in Kansas established, and that was in Leavenworth, more than 50 miles away. Topeka would have no public high school until 1870.

If Lincoln was going to offer higher education, it would first have to prepare students to receive it. As a result, all the students of the brand-new school enrolled in its preparatory department, which delivered essentially high-school-level courses.

Already, Lincoln had experienced plenty of birthing pains. The

Numbers

Population, 1870

- Kansas: 364,399
- Topeka: 5,790

Lincoln College, late 1860s.

first years of its life would continue to be a struggle — for attracting students and, as always, for attracting money.

Right away, a fundraising event

Most of the contributions made to establish Lincoln went into its endowment, which was supposed to remain untouched while it was invested to generate income. Up to and past school opening, however, the endowment generated only a pittance, and the trustees already had dipped into the principal to pay construction costs for the temporary building. Money was scarce even for furnishings.

"The farther I go from Topeka the greater the work before Lincoln College appears."

— Faculty member, upon his resignation

Supposedly, tuition would help pay for things, but in the early years Lincoln exempted many of the students — among them former Union soldiers and students intending to become ministers or schoolteachers. For students who did pay, the fee totaled $6 for the 11-week winter term.

Within weeks of school opening, the trustees staged a fundraiser, the Lincoln College Fair. The fair got under way at Lincoln's building on a windy, snowy mid-February evening. First came an oration — a popular entertainment of the day — followed by supper with music by a brass band. For the meal, the program promised "the best that the ladies of this city can furnish." Hundreds of people attended at 50 cents a head for a single evening, $1 for the full three days. The college offered for sale engravings, lithographs, photographs and collections of Bibles and picture albums.

A beautiful velvet album, the advertising promised, filled with pictures "and valued at $40 will be disposed of by ballot to the *handsomest* unmarried lady present." On the other hand, "a splendid engraving of President Johnson will be given in the same manner to the *homeliest* member of the Kansas Legislature."

The fair reportedly drew 500 people and cleared more than $600, which would be used to buy chairs and desks for the school.

But a fair was only the start. The trustees also decided to sell some of Lincoln's real estate. In addition, they appealed to a Connecticut-based group established to help institutions like Lincoln, the Society for the Promotion of Collegiate and Theological Education at the West — called the College Society for short. The trustees asked the society for $2,000 in direct aid, and also its blessing for a campaign to add tens of thousands of dollars to its endowment, mostly from New England.

Just getting by, the school finished its first term in late March with examinations and a

Lincoln College.

1865--66.

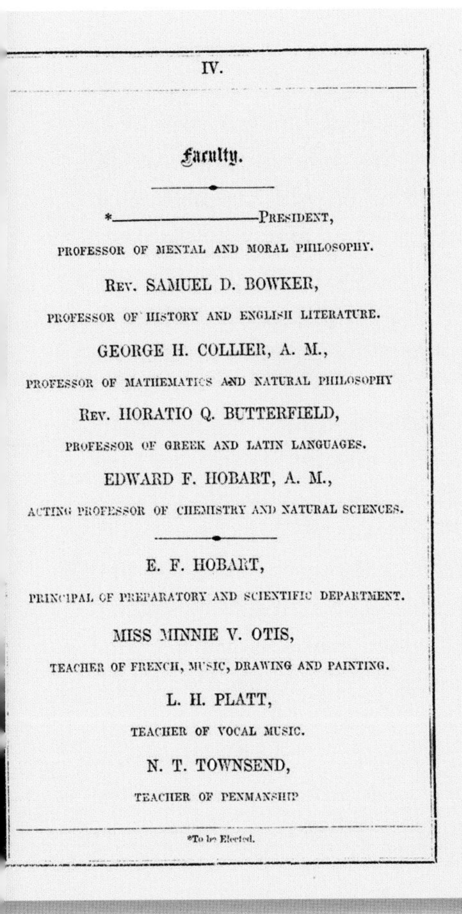

IV.

Faculty.

*—————— President,

PROFESSOR OF MENTAL AND MORAL PHILOSOPHY.

REV. SAMUEL D. BOWKER,

PROFESSOR OF HISTORY AND ENGLISH LITERATURE.

GEORGE H. COLLIER, A. M.,

PROFESSOR OF MATHEMATICS AND NATURAL PHILOSOPHY

REV. HORATIO Q. BUTTERFIELD,

PROFESSOR OF GREEK AND LATIN LANGUAGES.

EDWARD F. HOBART, A. M.,

ACTING PROFESSOR OF CHEMISTRY AND NATURAL SCIENCES.

E. F. HOBART,

PRINCIPAL OF PREPARATORY AND SCIENTIFIC DEPARTMENT.

MISS MINNIE V. OTIS,

TEACHER OF FRENCH, MUSIC, DRAWING AND PAINTING.

L. H. PLATT,

TEACHER OF VOCAL MUSIC.

N. T. TOWNSEND,

TEACHER OF PENMANSHIP

*To be Elected.

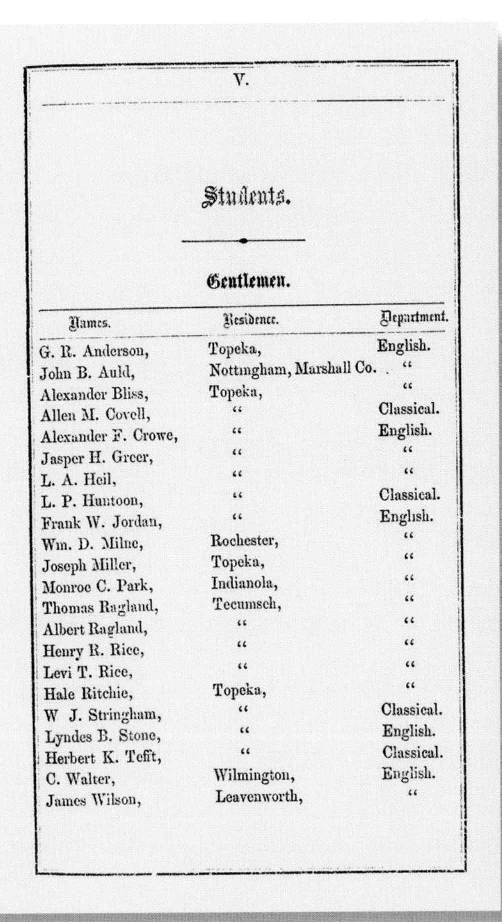

V.

Students.

Gentlemen.

Names.	Residence.	Department.
G. R. Anderson,	Topeka,	English.
John B. Auld,	Nottingham, Marshall Co.	"
Alexander Bliss,	Topeka,	"
Allen M. Covell,	"	Classical.
Alexander F. Crowe,	"	English.
Jasper H. Greer,	"	"
L. A. Heil,	"	"
L. P. Huntoon,	"	Classical.
Frank W. Jordan,	"	English.
Wm. D. Milne,	Rochester,	"
Joseph Miller,	Topeka,	"
Monroe C. Park,	Indianola,	"
Thomas Ragland,	Tecumseh,	"
Albert Ragland,	"	"
Henry R. Rice,	"	"
Levi T. Rice,	"	"
Hale Ritchie,	Topeka,	"
W J. Stringham,	"	Classical.
Lyndes B. Stone,	"	English.
Herbert K. Tefft,	"	Classical.
C. Walter,	Wilmington,	English.
James Wilson,	Leavenworth,	"

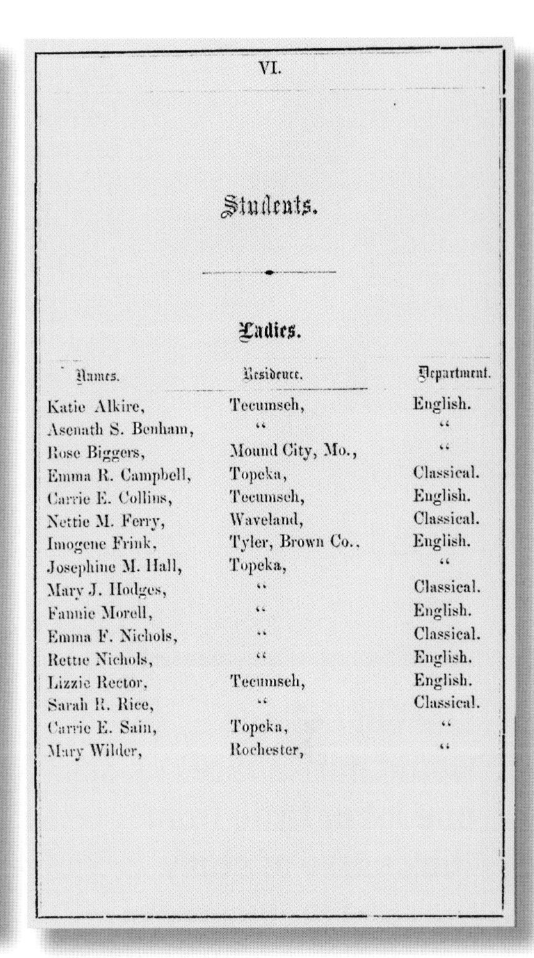

VI.

Students.

Ladies.

Names.	Residence.	Department.
Katie Alkire,	Tecumseh,	English.
Asenath S. Benham,	"	"
Rose Biggers,	Mound City, Mo.,	"
Emma R. Campbell,	Topeka,	Classical.
Carrie E. Collins,	Tecumseh,	English.
Nettie M. Ferry,	Waveland,	Classical.
Imogene Frink,	Tyler, Brown Co.,	English.
Josephine M. Hall,	Topeka,	"
Mary J. Hodges,	"	Classical.
Fannie Morell,	"	English.
Emma F. Nichols,	"	Classical.
Rettie Nichols,	"	English.
Lizzie Rector,	Tecumseh,	English.
Sarah R. Rice,	"	Classical.
Carrie E. Sain,	Topeka,	"
Mary Wilder,	Rochester,	"

The college's first catalog listed all the faculty and students on three pages. True to the founders' wishes, the roster of male students included an African-American. However, it did not identify which student he was.

public exhibition of some of its students' skills in oration, recitation and dialogue. At the end of the second term in June, one professor wished Lincoln well but, unable to keep his family housed and fed on his salary, resigned.

"The farther I go from Topeka the greater the work before Lincoln College appears," he wrote back. "It can scarcely take rank as a college for some years."

In May 1866, a committee of the College Society met in New Haven, Connecticut. Standing before it representing Lincoln was Samuel D. Bowker, who headed the preparatory department —the only department. He was assisted by Horatio Q. Butterfield, a 43-year-old New Englander, Harvard graduate and Congregational minister whom the trustees had worked hard to hire for the Lincoln faculty as a professor of Latin and Greek. The trustees won Butterfield's acceptance by allowing him to raise money for the college before he headed west. Some of the money Butterfield raised would supplement his own salary.

After hearing the case made by Bowker and Butterfield, the College Society members asked pointed questions.

Was Lincoln College authorized under Kansas law?

The necessary paperwork was brought forth.

Lincoln's bylaws called for its trustees to be acceptable to the General Association of Congregational Ministers and Churches of Kansas, so was the institution actually under ecclesiastical control?

No, the two professors argued, successfully.

Then came a more difficult question:

Where are the college-level students? The College Society, its members insisted, had not been formed to aid preparatory schools.

In fact, the College Society sympathized with the efforts of the Topeka school, and it set the bar low. Find three or two — or even one — freshman, and show that they were prepared for college, and the society would consider Lincoln a college and thus eligible for financial support.

Bowker and Butterfield reported this to Topeka, and the trustees went to work, looking for college-prepared youth wherever they could be mustered.

"All who are prepared to join the class are earnestly invited to send in their names at once," the college advertised.

Lincoln College would not "abate one jot or tittle from the course of study pursued in the great Universities of our land."

— Peter McVicar

Finally two young men, both of them Civil War veterans, stepped forward. One was Perley Griffin of Topeka, who had attended Harvard and now would enroll in Lincoln as a sophomore. The other was Addison P. Davis of Sarcoxie in nearby Jefferson County. Davis had gone to Beloit College in Wisconsin and would enter Lincoln as a junior.

With those two college-level students, Lincoln would become a college in fact as well as in name. The College Society committee announced that its requirements had been met.

"Resolved," the committee wrote, "That Lincoln College be received under the patronage of this Society and commended to the aid of the friends of Christian learning."

The trustees of Lincoln rejoiced and congratulated Bowker for his work. They also praised their own board president, Peter McVicar, who oversaw the effort to find and enroll the two students.

Higher education begins

On September 12, 1866, Lincoln began its third semester as an institution and its first as a college. The preparatory department would have 90 students. The college would have two.

The college students, in fact, would be outnumbered by the three members of the college faculty: Bowker, who taught English literature and grammar and who also was superintendent of the preparatory department; Butterfield, teaching Greek and Latin; and Minnie Otis, who taught French, music, drawing and painting.

And still the college had no president. Almost from its opening, the trustees had their eyes on Oliver Howard, a Union Army general who after the Civil War became commissioner of the Bureau of Refugees, Freedman and Abandoned Lands. The bureau was created in part to help freed slaves. Howard visited Topeka, but eventually he turned down Lincoln's offer. For the time being, the president of the Board of Trustees, Peter McVicar, continued to serve as de facto president of the college.

Before McVicar stepped down in December 1866 to serve as state superintendent of education, he reported to the General Association the good news that several students were preparing for the ministry and others for teaching. Lincoln College, he promised, would not "abate one jot or tittle from the course of study pursued in the great universities of our land."

McVicar was succeeded as head of the trustees by Lewis Bodwell, who had once again taken the reins of the local Congregational Church.

Then came more worries. Despite Lincoln's having enrolled college-level students, the College Society in Connecticut had not come through with money. The trustees began borrowing to meet faculty payroll. They faced down an attempt by interests in Leavenworth, then the largest city in the region, to move the college there. They debated whether the 160 acres deeded by Ritchie for a permanent

Peter McVicar: Dedicated to the "new college on the frontier"

He was as much a minister as an educator, and believed that Bible study went hand-in-hand with traditional educational study. Peter McVicar was just what a Christian-founded college wanted.

"The religious motive," he said in 1887, "was the inspiring motive in the founding of Washburn College and continues today as the life force of the enterprise."

McVicar was an imposing figure, standing six feet three inches tall and weighing 250 pounds.

"Wherever he appeared," one faculty member recalled, "he attracted general attention."

McVicar was born in New Brunswick, in Canada, of parents who emigrated from Scotland. One associate recalled that his speech never completely lost its Scottish burr. McVicar spent his teenage years in Wisconsin, where his parents had moved to farm, and he graduated from Beloit College. He finished theological training in 1860 at Andover seminary in Massachusetts, where anti-slavery enthusiasm and concern for the Kansas statehood question had burned brightly through the decade.

In October 1860, he arrived in Topeka and the next May became pastor of the Congregational Church, replacing Lewis Bodwell, who had enlisted with a missionary group. On February 1, 1871, after serving as state superintendent of education, McVicar was chosen president of Washburn.

McVicar was sympathetic in his attitude toward others, another faculty member recalled years later, yet dignified and somewhat reserved: "There was something about him that kept people at a respectful distance."

"There was something about him that kept people at a respectful distance."

His jokes "were brief and almost apologetic," another professor remembered, and he showed his humor only by a twinkle in his eye.

Every student got to know McVicar as a teacher because all Washburn students took his classes in mental and moral philosophy, political economy and evidences of Christianity. One student remembered McVicar as "a theologian of the old school seemingly never bothered by a doubt."

Many students found him daunting and sometimes difficult to understand as a person.

"Dr. McVicar possessed a poise and dignity which discouraged approach by the average undergraduate," recalled an alumnus in 1932. "I doubt if he knew how to become a confidante of his students."

In student publications, he was often referred to as "The Doctor."

Distant or not, no one could question McVicar's dedication to building "a new college on the frontier," as one alumnus put it.

"Fortunately for the institution, he brought to it the devotion, the zeal, the patience and determination that were needed for the endless task of finding funds to build up the college and carry on its work," the alumnus, Frank A. Quail, said. "It seems safe to say that no contribution to Washburn has ever been made...that could compare in value with the pioneer work of Dr. McVicar."

Peter McVicar died June 5, 1903.

Today, the street that bears his name and marks the western boundary of the Washburn campus is spelled "MacVicar." Possibly, the spelling change resulted from a mistake made when the campus chapel was named for McVicar in 1902. A stone placed above the doorway used the "Mac" spelling. Both spellings appeared in newspaper accounts of the early 20th century in reference to McVicar and to his adult children.

President's on-campus residence, probably 1880s.

Horatio Q. Butterfield

campus was close enough to town, considered several parcels that were nearer and then wound up sticking with the 160 acres.

They lost Samuel Bowker, the hard-working fundraiser, teacher and administrator, who resigned because of "impaired health" and who would die of tuberculosis in early 1868. Lincoln College, they said, owed "its existence, in large degree to his faith and industry."

In March 1867, Lincoln made Horatio Q. Butterfield its financial agent, or chief fundraiser, for a year and he headed back east, where the money was.

By May of that year, the need for cash was so desperate that the trustees discussed shutting down some or all of Lincoln's operations. By July 1867 the financial report was stark. In the preceding academic year, Lincoln had brought in a little less than $1,600. It had spent more than $4,500.

Lewis Bodwell, now president of the trustees, wrote Butterfield about Lincoln's rising debt:

"So great have been its dangers that we have talked of curtailing. But where?"

Shutting down the preparatory department would not help, Bodwell wrote, because "it near or quite pays its own way."

The problem was the college. Despite, or perhaps because of, its tiny enrollment the college came nowhere near paying its own way. Yet the college — and its promise of preparing students for the ministry — was the reason Lincoln existed.

Butterfield would have to come up with something.

As summer 1867 turned to fall and the beginning of a new academic year, the trustees crossed another hurdle and achieved another mark set for them by the College Society: Lincoln was to have a freshman class. It would contain four Topeka men and another man from Doniphan County in northeast Kansas. Together with Addison Davis, now a senior, and Perley Griffin, a junior, college-level enrollment totaled seven.

Meanwhile, Butterfield scoured New England for contributions and began to find them. He worked to collect money not only for the endowment but also for day-to-day operations. By January 1868, Butterfield had collected enough to pay off what was owed to the faculty. In Kansas, Lincoln received gifts of land and several thousand dollars in cash.

The end of that academic year, June 1868, saw the first commencement of Lincoln College. Graduation exercises — featuring music, prayer, more music, orations and yet more music — took place in late June at the Congregational Church.

Addison P. Davis became the first graduate of Lincoln College. He gave an oration entitled "The Tendency of Cities," and was encouraged by Bodwell, the trustees' president, to set an example for those graduates who came after him.

At commencement one year later, Perley

PROGRAMME

OF THE

FIRST COMMENCEMENT

OF

LINCOLN COLLEGE.

EXERCISES COMMENCING

SUNDAY EVENING, JUNE 21ST.

CLOSING

WEDNESDAY EVENING, JUNE 24TH,

1868.

PROGRAMME.

SUNDAY EVENING, JUNE 21st.

7 1-2 P. M.—Address before the Missionary Society of Inquiry, Rev. J. D. LIGGETT.

MONDAY, JUNE 22d.

Nine A. M. and One P. M.—Annual Examination.

TUESDAY, JUNE 23d.

Nine A. M. and One P. M.—Examination Continued.
7 1-2 P. M.—Oration before the Ciceronian Society, Rev. RICHARD CORDLEY.

WEDNESDAY, JUNE 24th.

Commencement Exercises beginning Nine A. M.

Music--Prayer--Music.

Oration.—Labor versus Genius, ... W. I. STRINGHAM.
Oration.—Self Culture, ... L. P. HUNTOON.
Oration.—Imperfections of Our Government, ... J. B. BILLARD.

Music.

Oration.—Consistency, ... M. R. MOORE.
Essay.—Home Influences, ... Miss CARRIE SAIN.
Essay.—Born to Die, ... Miss HATTIE D. SCALES.

Music.

Oration.—Discipline of the Classics, ... P. M. GRIFFIN.
Oration.—The Tendency of Cities, ... A. P. DAVIS.

Music.

Baccalaureate—Conferring Degrees.

Music.

BENEDICTION.

WEDNESDAY EVENING.

REUNION.

Millison & Co. Print, Topeka.

Griffin got his degree, as did Hattie Scales, the first woman graduate. Nationwide economic problems in the 1870s reduce the number of graduates, but eventually, there would be many. Addison P. Davis however, was the only one whose diploma read "Lincoln College."

The benefactor

That fall, Butterfield's fundraising mission to the East took him to a resident of Worcester, Massachusetts, whose company manufactured wire.

Ichabod Washburn had found ways to produce wire efficiently and in large volume and the result for him was a great fortune. Washburn became a deacon in the Congregational church and a munificent donor to schools, churches and hospitals. Butterfield hoped the odds were good that Washburn would look kindly on his entreaties on behalf of Lincoln College.

Those hopes were realized.

In late October 1868, Washburn told Butterfield he would give the struggling college in Topeka $25,000 — a stunning amount in those days. Washburn's money would nearly double the assets of the college.

One thing was necessary in return. Butterfield reported to the trustees that the College Society and others interested in Lincoln's future believed it would be fitting to rename the college after Ichabod Washburn.

Considering the gift a godsend, the trustees of Lincoln College did not hesitate. On November 19, they decided that there already were too many "literary institutions" in the United States named after Abraham Lincoln and renamed the fledgling Topeka institution for its biggest benefactor.

"We express our hearty thanks to Deacon Washburn," the trustees said in their resolution, "coming as it does in the infancy of our enterprise and assuring its success. We trust... our College may be an honor to its donors and

College namesake

The man whose name was taken by Washburn College never went to college. Ichabod Washburn, a devout Congregationalist, always regretted that, and contributed hundreds of thousands of dollars to American colleges and churches. He believed all people, including women and minorities, had a right to an education.

Ichabod Washburn. Below: his factory in Worcester, Massachusetts.

Ichabod Washburn was born August 11, 1798, in Kingston, Massachusetts. His father was a sea captain who died when Ichabod was two months old, leaving him, his twin brother and a 4-year-old sister to be raised by their mother. As a boy, Ichabod Washburn was apprenticed to a harness-maker and, as a teenager, to a blacksmith. Then he began building a successful career out of various ways of forming metal, first manufacturing lead pipe with a partner.

In 1831 Washburn began making wire. He found ways to vastly improve the efficiency of machinery that drew wire from steel rods, and thus fed an American market for wire that was growing yearly. In 1850 he developed a way to make steel-wire piano strings and later entered the business of making wire for the then-fashionable hoop skirts.

His Washburn and Moen (for his son-in-law and partner, Phillip Moen) Wire Works in Worcester, Massachusetts — about 40 miles west of downtown Boston — grew to a workforce of 700 by 1868, the year Washburn died at the age of 70.

1866-1901

1866: On January 3, Lincoln College opened its doors. — In September, the first two college-level students enrolled at Lincoln. **1868:** Ichabod Washburn of Worcester, Massachusetts, contributed $25,000 and the college was renamed after him. **1869:** Horatio Q. Butterfield, who persuaded Washburn to make his donation, became the first president of the college. **1871:** Peter McVicar was named president. **1874:** Washburn moved to its new campus southwest of Topeka. **1884:** A horse- and mule-drawn streetcar line reached campus from the city. **1885:** *The Washburn Argo*, first student publication at the college, appeared.

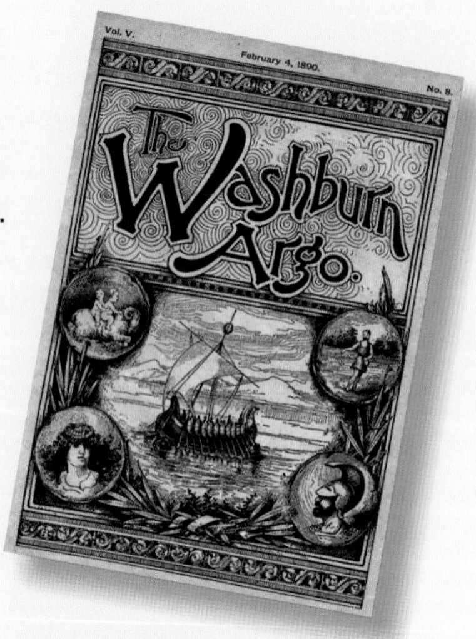

a blessing to our state."

And so the one-building school in Topeka became Washburn College.

Ichabod Washburn never saw the institution that had been named after him. On December 30, barely two months after making his donation, he died of complications from a stroke.

Years later, Richard Cordley, a prominent Congregational minister in Lawrence and backer of Lincoln/Washburn College, recalled how important the gift of the New England industrialist had been.

"It came at a critical time and marked an era in our history," Cordley said. "The work had gone about as far as it could without larger resources.

"Money men ... are shy of institutions which need their gifts to make them secure. Mr. Washburn gave his magnificent gift at the beginning when most men shrink. Mr. Washburn had the rare faith to see the promise in an enterprise not yet assured to mortal sight. The college had an endowment, and its perpetuity was ensured."

thus creating confusion and embarrassing us
in our movements — and
Whereas Dea. I. Washburne of Worcester, Mass.
proposes to make to our College a donation
of Twenty five thousand dollars towards the endowment we are seeking — Therefore
Resolved That we, the Trustees of Lincoln College —
in a meeting legally called, and assembling
at Topeka this nineteenth day of November
One Thousand Eight hundred and Sixty eight
do hereby Change the name of said Institution to Washburne College.
Resolved — That we express our hearty thanks to Dea. Washburne, for his generous gift — coming as it does

From the Board of Trustees record, the official renaming of the college after Ichabod Washburn.

Estimating the worth of Washburn's $25,000 in 21st-century dollars is difficult, but a conservative estimate might put it at $1 million. There might have been even more help from Ichabod Washburn, perhaps as much as $75,000 more, according to a statement by the college president in 1890, if not for his death.

The other hero of the day was the man who elicited the donation: Horatio Q. Butterfield. Recognizing that, seven months after his fundraising coup that kept the newborn college afloat, the Board of Trustees chose Butterfield to become the first president of the renamed college. On June 25, 1869, Butterfield accepted their offer.

With the capable Reverend Butterfield at the helm, the new Washburn College appeared to be set for a few years without financial distress.

Yet in November 1870, only 17 months after taking over as president, Butterfield submitted his resignation to go to work for the College Society in Connecticut, the same group to which he had helped present the college's pleas for money. The trustees turned their attention to Cordley, pastor of Plymouth Congregational Church in Lawrence, as Butterfield's successor. But on December 20, Butterfield withdrew his resignation and the choice of Cordley was set aside.

Forty-one days after that, on January 20,

1887: The federal government established a weather station at Washburn's Main or Science building. Topeka's weather records began there. In 1892 the office was moved downtown.

1890: Washburn played its first recognized football game. It lost, 32-0, to Baker University.

1894: The term schedule was changed from three terms of three months each to two semesters, each four and one-half months long.

– In February, Washburn students helped National Guardsmen enforce order during the battle between Populists and Republicans over control of the Kansas Legislature.

1895: First yearbook, *The Helianthus*, appeared.

1896: Electricity arrived on campus.

– George Herrick was named president.

1897: On February 4, *The Washburn Review*, successor to several earlier student newspapers, began publication.

– Horatio Q. Butterfield, who in 1868 persuaded Ichabod Washburn to donate $25,000, died.

– A baseball game against St. Mary's was canceled after objections to Washburn's having a black player.

1901: George Herrick stepped down as president.

– Washburn women organized the first basketball team at the college for either sex.

1871, Butterfield sent the trustees a telegram from New York. Once more he was resigning, this time for good. He joined the College Society. In 1876 he would move to the presidency of Mount Olivet College in Michigan.

Events were twisting and turning rapidly and Washburn, the little college that had struggled so often in its early years, faced yet another decision: its next leader. This time the trustees made a move that stuck. It would bring consistent leadership for the next quarter-century.

On the outskirts of town

In February 1871, the trustees named as president Peter McVicar, who was no stranger to the struggles of the college.

As chairman of the first Board of Trustees in the mid-1860s, McVicar had been involved in its founding. He also had been superintendent of schools in Shawnee County and later the state of Kansas. McVicar was an ordained minister who for six years, from 1860 to 1866, had been pastor of the Congregational Church in Topeka.

Soon after McVicar assumed the presidency, the school began planning its move to the long-promised permanent campus on the 160-acre tract southwest of town. McVicar would preside over its construction.

As the 1870s began, drought and grasshoppers plagued Kansas farmers and severely damaged business in the young state. A financial panic in 1873 depressed the entire national economy. More than ever, finding money would prove a chore but McVicar and the trustees went to work.

In June 1871, the college made a proposal to the City of Topeka and its school board. Washburn would turn over its temporary building and grounds at 10th and Jackson to the city, and would give tuition breaks to qualified youth of Topeka, in return for the city's issuing $15,000 in bonds with which Washburn would start its new campus. In a special election, the voters of Topeka said yes.

A renewed fundraising effort drew $25,000 in pledges. Costs eventually would exceed $55,000. The money "for erection of the first college building," McVicar later said, "can be accounted for only by the recognition

A day of classes in 1869, sandwiched between morning and afternoon devotions.

Baseball was the first organized sport at Washburn, beginning in 1879. This was the 1898-99 team.

of a special and divine agency."

McVicar probably was being too modest. Richard Cordley, the man originally elected to succeed Butterfield, credited McVicar's considerable personal skills with persuading donors to part with money. McVicar, he wrote in 1890, showed foresight and "the acquaintance and confidence of the businessmen of Topeka." Also, McVicar was blessed with "tact, patience and perseverance."

J.G. Haskell, designer of the new Kansas Capitol, was hired as architect. He drew up plans for a single structure 130 feet long, 54 feet wide and four stories tall.

Work began in June 1872 under the supervision of Harvey Rice and the building was enclosed a year later, but construction was slowed by the recession of the early 1870s. Evidently, some in the General Association asked why the college did not delay construction until the economy recovered. To that, McVicar replied:

"It is always easier to keep an object moving than to start it after it has once stopped."

Putting an exclamation point on his pleas for contributions, McVicar turned down part of his salary and made a donation to the building fund.

For decades, wealthy New Englanders would help keep Washburn afloat and growing, thanks to McVicar. He hired a Massachusetts minister to scout New England for potential contributors with instructions to keep an eye out for parents who had lost children and might consider giving money to Washburn as a memorial. McVicar followed up by making extended trips to the East, seeking contributions immediately or in the donors' wills.

In October 1873 came news that the college had awaited since before it was renamed. The College Society of Connecticut finally would send money, about $2,300. The money must be returned, the society said, if Washburn ceased to be a Christian college or it "became subject to political or ecclesiastical control."

In the exchange with the city of Topeka, the original building at 10th and Jackson streets was turned into a public school, so Washburn cast about for classroom space until construction was finished at its new campus. In the 1872-1873 academic year, Washburn held classes in a grocery building and in 1873-74 in a building at the corner of Eighth and Kansas.

Finally, in 1874, Washburn College opened its doors on the site where it would remain — the gentle rise outside the city limits, which became known as College Hill. The lone building contained everything there was. On the first floor were classrooms, the library and a chapel. On the second and third floors were dormitory rooms for students and the college offices. The basement contained a kitchen, and dining and meeting rooms.

Washburn's 160 acres encompassed bare prairie, so McVicar busied himself arranging for plantings. He enclosed 40 acres with a fence and hedge of Osage Orange, and within that portion planted elms and cottonwoods.

In 1876, Washburn's main building was its only building. The entire college existed inside it.

The stone structure would be called Main Building and then Science Building and later Old Science until after the turn of the 20th century, when it would formally be named Rice Hall after Harvey Rice.

In its first five years the structure needed no name: it was the only building on campus. The second was Hartford Cottage, a women's dormitory, named for the city and surroundings from where most of its contributions had come — Hartford, Connecticut. Residents of the cottage, besides attending classes, were to spend one hour a day doing household work.

Hartford Cottage, second building on campus. It served as a women's dormitory.

The campus lay more than a mile past the city limit, and at first horse-drawn stages called "omnibuses" and later horse- and mule-drawn streetcars brought men and women to class — if they did not walk.

Despite McVicar's efforts at tree-plant-

The first library building, Boswell, and its reading room, below.

ing, newcomers still found the campus rather barren. One such newcomer arrived in 1878, four years after the college moved to its permanent site. He was J.T. Lovewell, a Yale Ph.D. who was joining the faculty, of which he would be a member for 22 years. Lovewell reached north Topeka on the Union Pacific Railroad.

"My conveyance out to Washburn was a sort of express wagon," Lovewell recalled. "I rode for a long distance and came to a lone building ... in the north part of a field ... which was surrounded by Osage Orange hedge. Around the hedge had been built a board fence to protect the hedge from cattle herds grazing on the prairie."

Life at Washburn

Washburn students came mainly from Topeka, which by 1890 surpassed 35,000 in population, and from Shawnee County. In addition to Hartford Cottage, the college built several more dormitories, but plenty of students lived with family in town, or in boarding houses.

Recognizing that many prospective students could not afford the full cost of college, Washburn made scholarships available "through the generosity of friends at the East." Testimonials signed by "two or three responsible citizens of their locality" were required. Part-time work was encouraged.

"Anyone who is bent on securing an education will usually be able to afford it," Washburn said in its catalog. "The old maxim holds true... as in everything else, that 'Where there is a will there is a way.'"

There were ways to spread the faculty's efforts, too. The newly arrived J.T. Lovewell's specialties were chemistry and physics but he would also teach Latin, Greek, German, French, astronomy and political science.

In 1878, his first year on the job, Lovewell recalled, Washburn had 25 college students and three instructors besides McVicar, and the president spent much of his time in the East trying to raise money.

The college catalog of 1878-1879 gave a sampling of classes conducted in the collegiate course. Freshmen, sophomores and juniors studied Latin and Greek each year with doses of algebra, geometry, trigonometry and physics. Seniors added astronomy and geology, mental and moral philosophy and logic. In all but one semester of every year, students were required to take classes in rhetoric, including orations, compositions, essays and themes. A college-level "scientific

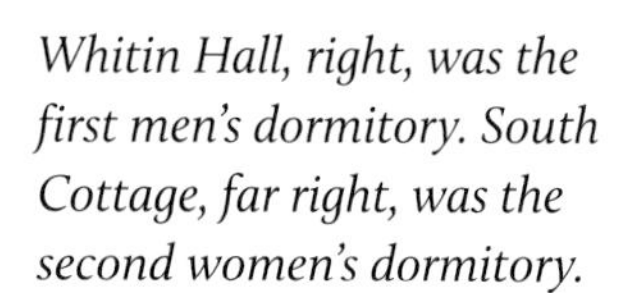

Whitin Hall, right, was the first men's dormitory. South Cottage, far right, was the second women's dormitory.

course" substituted natural science courses for the rhetoric requirements.

As a Congregationalist-founded school, Washburn required regular chapel attendance. Much of the faculty came from ministerial ranks. In the late 1870s, daily devotional services were held each morning with evening services on Wednesdays.

The Congregationalists did not dictate that students follow their doctrine. On Sunday mornings, students were required to attend services, but they could do so at any church. Although religious affiliation was common among Washburn students, a substantial number of them represented Christian denominations other than Congregational.

Discipline was strict on campus. Dancing, alcohol, tobacco — even dating — were frowned upon or prohibited.

Faculty rules on social conduct, as recalled by one student of the early 1880s, were, "in the sight of most of the boys (and many of the girls) unmercifully severe. Communication and association, except within certain narrow limitations, was forbidden."

Women students, it was thought, required special treatment. The 1884-1885 catalog recommended that "parents arrange the time of leaving home that their daughters may reach Topeka by day," presumably to prevent any night-walking characters from preying on them.

At least some of the students appreciated faculty efforts. An 1880 resident of Hartford Cottage recalled the new cottage preceptress, Carrie L. White, as a "strong woman of infinite tact" who "soon won the hearts of her more or less untrained houseful of young girls."

Competitive juices

Student energies were channeled into so-called literary societies, which encouraged skill in using words, spoken and written. Years afterward Topeka lawyer Robert Stone,

Amid books and photos, senior women threw a party in the 1890s. Below: Cast of the class play, "Der Neffe als Onkel" (The Nephew as Uncle), about 1899.

Frances Storrs

Lucy Platt Harshbarger

Washburn's alma mater began in the mind of Frederic Phelps, a professor of Greek and Latin. Phelps had a favorite melody that he could hum but not name. He liked the tune enough to ask a student, Frances Storrs, to write lyrics for it. Another student, the musically inclined Lucy Platt Harshbarger, heard him hum the same melody, and transcribed and harmonized it. With the lyrics, the result was known for years only as the Washburn Song. It became the college alma mater in the 1930s. Storrs graduated in 1892.

an 1889 Washburn graduate, recalled how his friends and he had formed the Gamma Sigma Literary Society, which originated the first college paper, *The Washburn Argo*, a monthly. The next academic year, 1886-1887, a competing weekly was begun called *The Reporter*. Opposing factions operated each paper, which "gave zest to college life" in the lawyer's recollection. *The Reporter*'s creed was simple: "Fight the *Argo*."

The mental jousting apparently strengthened Washburn students' debating and speaking skills. Beginning in the mid-1880s, Washburn students won four state oratorical contests in five years.

Not until the turn of the century would athletics, powered by the popularity of football, displace forensics as the leading competitive activity.

In the late 19th century, baseball dominated newspaper sports sections and every community had a team. Baseball also dominated sporting activities at Washburn, but only toward the end of the academic year, once spring arrived. One student of the early 1880s recalled a diamond "crudely laid out" south of South Cottage. Home plate was made of a building stone lifted from a campus construction project and buried.

Football would not begin to take hold until the 1890s, basketball had not been invented and no track team existed.

How it grew

When Peter McVicar entered office in 1871, the college over which he presided listed two juniors and six freshmen. The next year, college-level enrollment reached nine. Enrollment in the preparatory department — the courses at high school-level courses — hovered in the middle 40s. Not until the 1883-1884 academic year did total enrollment of college and preparatory students surpass 200.

As the years went by, the preparatory department continued to represent the majority of Washburn students. In 1886, the number of college-level students had grown substantially, yet only 35 were counted among a total enrollment of 241. Twenty years had passed since the opening of Kansas' first public high school in Leavenworth, but college-prepared students remained few in number. Washburn's preparatory level had to continue for the foreseeable future, the school catalog said, "owing to the lack of secondary schools in sufficient number, and of the proper goals, to fit students for collegiate classes."

In 1892, the preparatory department was renamed the Academy, and once again received its own principal. The reason given was that the work done by the Academy and the college had become almost entirely distinct from one another.

Little by little, the built portion of campus grew, too.

In 1880, a home for President McVicar was added. In that year, Topeka celebrated Arbor Day and Washburn students were enlisted to plant trees.

On a journey to Boston in 1884, McVicar stopped in West Hartford, Connecticut, to visit Charles Boswell at Boswell's invitation. After McVicar gave a talk at Boswell's church, Boswell gave him a pledge of $10,000 for a new library. Boswell proved to be a good friend to Washburn over the years, and in his estate he made the college a legatee. Because of restrictions in Boswell's will, the largest amount would take half a century to ripen into an actual donation.

In the middle 1880s a New Englander named J.C. Whitin died, instructing his heirs to send Washburn $10,000. McVicar had tried to visit Whitin, but failed each time, and was surprised when money came through anyway. The funds enabled Washburn to build a second women's dormitory, South Cottage, and a men's dormitory, Whitin Hall.

Among Washburn graduates in the class of 1882 were Cora Kirby Sellards, above, and Mary Sherrill Smith.

Holbrook Hall residents, about 1899.

In 1884, Topeka and Washburn were connected by a streetcar line powered by mules. The line, which began at the Santa Fe Depot and ended at Washburn, made nine trips a day. In 1889, it was electrified and by 1891 two electric-powered streetcar lines served the campus.

Middle 1885 brought money for yet another women's dormitory, supported by a gift from Mary Holbrook of Holbrook, Massachusetts.

At McVicar's urging the school had also purchased a 135-acre tract adjoining the north side of campus. For decades afterward it generated income through the sale or lease of lots. The property, which what would become known as the College Hill neighborhood, also served as a way to attract faculty, to whom lots could be deeded by the trustees.

Through the heady economic days of the 1880s, McVicar floated proposals for new enterprises. One was for a school of mining and mining engineering, probably encouraged by the gold and silver strikes in the West. Another was a campus arboretum. Yet another was a department of meteorological observation.

Boswell and Holbrook halls were dedicated in 1886, and at the ceremony

Holbrook Hall, above, and its residents, facing page. Right, top, a parlor inside Holbrook in 1886, the year it opened. Bottom, a student room, replete with "W" banner and plenty of pillows.

Faculty and administration, President George Herrick at center, 1899-1900.

President McVicar thanked the donors:

"If it were not for the generous friends at the East, and the many friends in Kansas who from time to time contributed so liberally to the work, the College could not have succeeded."

One set of friends who had not been nearly so generous with money, McVicar pointed out gently, were Kansas Congregational churches, which were "not able to aid largely in a pecuniary point of view." He hoped they could be of more help "as the years go on, and the means increase within the bounds of the state." They did win a compliment from him for sending "their sons and daughters" as students.

In 1890 the college opened a 700-seat chapel, a $40,000 structure that held religious exercises and school meetings, rooms for student religious groups and general lecture rooms.

End of an era

As times changed, as the college became more complex and as more students enrolled, the administration and trustees faced a never-ending need to enlarge the endowment and find money any way they could.

"Our teachers are poorly paid," wrote Trustee Richard Cordley in 1890, the 25th anniversary of Washburn's founding, "and we cannot offer to increase their compensation."

Deficits piled up — $7,400 in 1890, nearly $12,500 in 1891 and $15,000 in 1892. In 1893, combined income from tuition and from interest on the $67,000 endowment totaled $13,500 but spending surpassed $18,000.

In 1894, McVicar reported to the trustees that Washburn continued to run a deficit, and no grand bequests lay in sight. The college could send an agent out to raise $5,000. Or it could find 100 more students, which at $40 a year would produce $4,000. Or it could add $50,000 to the endowment, which at 7 percent interest would yield $3,500.

None of that would be easy.

Real estate investments in Kansas had begun to decline after 1888, and in 1893 a nationwide recession slowed the economy to a crawl. Over the years, Washburn had accumulated farm properties, many of them in Wabaunsee County, the next county west of Topeka and Shawnee County. The property generated income through mortgages, but in slow times strapped farmers fell behind on their payments or defaulted entirely. Taxes on the land did not go away and, as owner, the college was the final taxpayer.

With the declining economy came declining enrollments. In 1894, McVicar told the trustees that total enrollment had dropped from 293 the preceding year to 264.

Through his long tenure as president, Peter McVicar raised money like a champion.

But even he had his limit.

In 1895, when McVicar turned 66 years old, the trustees set out on a new campaign to add $50,000 to the endowment. Worn down by decades of pleading with donors, McVicar decided to step down. Officially, his term ended in August 1896, although because of ill health he was inactive for much of the year before.

Fifteen years later, one of McVicar's successors would say that in McVicar's tenure "the affairs of Washburn College were about as complicated as those of our academy, and standards were very little higher."

Yet McVicar was revered as few other presidents have been, and among Washburn presidents he still holds the record for tenure, 25 years. In his honor, the campus chapel was named for him in 1902, along with the street that forms Washburn's western boundary.

New president, same tasks

In June 1896, the trustees hired George M. Herrick of Chicago as McVicar's replacement. The Vermont-born Herrick had graduated from Beloit College in Wisconsin, also McVicar's alma mater. He had spent several years in public-school administration in Illinois and two years with the New West Education society, a Congregational-supported group that merged with the College Society. The mission of the group was to promote Christian education in the newer, western states of the Union, and Herrick spoke regularly on the subject. Unlike Washburn's first two presidents, Herrick was not a minister.

According to several accounts, Herrick relaxed the relationship between the students and the faculty and administration, loosening some of the tight discipline for which McVicar was known.

In academic matters, he hired Washburn's first sociology professor — and one of the first in that field in the United States — Daniel Moses Fisk. Another prominent hire was Charlotte Leavitt, an English instructor who would remain at Washburn for 40 years, retiring as a full professor.

The chapel, built in 1890, eventually would be named for Peter McVicar.

Herrick would be president only five years, and he spent much of his final three years away from Topeka. Indeed, for Washburn Day celebrations in February 1899, Herrick was in New England and sent a telegram. He had left Topeka January 7 to visit Chicago, New York and Boston "in the interest of the college," meaning to try to raise money. He was not expected back until May 1.

For the last three years of Herrick's term, according to a 1901 account in *The Topeka Daily Capital*, Professor Frederick W. Ellis had served as acting president "in the absence of President George M. Herrick."

In spring 1901 Herrick resigned. Rumors of friction between Herrick and the Board of Trustees were heard at the time, although both sides denied it. By that year, the board had 18 members, compared with 12 when Lincoln College was chartered. All were men, and five were clergymen. As late as 1897, the body still had three members who served on the original board in 1865 — McVicar, Harvey Rice and Richard Cordley.

For his part, Herrick said that fundrais-

Following pages: Staff of The Washburn Mid Continent, *an early student newspaper.*

THE WASHBVRN
MID-CONTINENT

The Washburn . . .

Weekly Review.

Vol. XIII. February 4, 1897. No. 20.

OFFICIAL Organ of the State Oratorical Association. + + + +

THE Washburn Mid-Continent, Established 1885. The Washburn Reporter, Established 1887. Consolidated into "The Washburn Weekly Review" in 1897.

Washburn College, + +

+ + Topeka, Kansas.

First issue of The Review, *1897.*

ing had been unpleasant and his work in that field unappreciated. He told *The Capital* that he had come to Washburn with an agreement that he would also teach, and "did not care" to continue soliciting money. Evidently, however, he had done well at it; the trustees reported that 1900-1901 had been a prosperous year.

Herrick also chided Kansans for not "supporting Washburn as they should." In addition, he said Washburn lost friends because of reports that a group of students and professors had joined Carrie Nation and scores of others on a "smashing tour" of Topeka bars and liquor storage houses in February 1901.

The end of his term coincided with the beginning of the 20th century. Herrick left academe and went into the insurance business in Chicago.

Few records remain from Herrick's tenure, but in a farewell essay that he wrote for *The Washburn Review* he said he had given "the best five years of my life" to the college, and proudly stated, "I am sure that we can all rejoice in the evident and substantial increase which the last five years has seen."

At the final commencement over which he presided in 1901 were 21 graduates, nine women and 12 men. In the fall semester of 1901, Washburn enrolled a little more than 300 students at college level and 128 in the Academy. The endowment stood at about $70,000 and the annual budgeted spending was just under $30,000. Faculty totaled 23 members.

Compared with 10, 20 or 30 years before, those were big numbers. But they were nothing compared with what lay just over the horizon in the opening years of the 20th century.

Walter Caldwell, enrolled in Washburn's newly acquired Medical School, played halfback on the 1903 team that won seven games, lost none and tied one, and also won the Kansas Conference championship. The Kansas City Medics were denounced by The Review, *facing page, for refusing to play Washburn because of Caldwell's presence.*

In the northwest section of campus, Washburn fenced off an area and built bleachers for football games.

Football, in the beginning

An early form of football, inspired by an English rugby player who worked in the railroad shops in Topeka, was played at Washburn as early as 1885, but the ball was rounder than today's and potential opponents were few. In 1886, *The Argo* reported that the University of Kansas football club challenged Washburn to a game. None took place, however, supposedly because KU withdrew over a lack of practice time. An earlier match in Lawrence was called off when KU did not show up.

By 1890, Washburn played Baker College of Baldwin City in football, but lost 32-0. In 1891, Washburn, Baker and KU formed a Triangular League. The first game took place November 7, 1891, between Baker and Washburn at Baldwin City and again Baker won. KU won the league, beating Washburn and Baker twice each.

Leagues came and went and foes changed yearly. Ottawa University joined high school teams and the YMCA on Washburn's schedule.

Recruiting complaints surfaced often. Accusations that some teams hired professional players were fired back and forth. In 1897 and 1899, some opponents refused to play Washburn because its team included black players.

The 1900 Washburn football team, coached by Bennie Owen, was one of the early era's best. It beat KU twice, 24-0 and 29-0, and split two games against Haskell. Its only other loss was to the Denver Athletic Club. Owen left after only one year to become an assistant coach at the University of Michigan and eventually head coach at the University of Oklahoma.

Washburn's 1898 football team.

Washburn Review — Oct. 2, 1903

Caldwell Plays or No Game.

Manager Leach of the football team has received communication from the K. C. Medics to the effect that they will play Washburn October 24th, provided no colored men are in the game. Although the financial consideration was fair, and although if played the game would draw an excellent crowd, Manager Leach flatly refused to play unless this restriction was withdrawn. The manager's policy is to be heartily commended by students and faculty.

It has always been a custom in Washburn to recognize neither color nor class. This is one of the fundamental principles on which she was founded. The brotherhood of man is her slogan. That this principle be violated on the athletic field is folly.

When Washburn goes to Missouri to play, the time honored customs of the inhabitants of that state are respected, and when Missourians come to Kansas it is no more than right that the customs of the Jayhawkers be so honored. Anyone can see that it would be to the Medics advantage to deprive us of Caldwell for he is a star and they know it, but what is more important than that he is a man and we know it.

1902-1918

New Momentum

For its first three and one-half decades, Washburn College hummed along, providing a liberal arts education to a few score college students each year and preparing a few hundred younger people to go to college. With the arrival of the 20th century, the little institution on the outskirts of Topeka burst forth with new buildings, new schools and new majors, climbing enrollments and an expanding endowment.

Seemingly overnight, Washburn transformed itself into a multidimensional institution. First came a new School of Fine Arts in summer 1902. In October, the 12-year-old Kansas Medical College of Topeka agreed to merge with Washburn. In September 1903, Washburn began its own School of Law in downtown Topeka.

All this turn-of-the-century momentum was driven by its new and hard-charging president, a man whom one historian dubbed "entrepreneurial." The word fit; in many ways he resembled an eager innovator overseeing a startup business.

Numbers

Population, 1910

- Kansas: 1,690,949
- Topeka: 43,684

Off and running

Norman Plass joined the Washburn ranks in 1901 as field secretary, a fundraising position. He began paying visits to potential donors in New England before he ever saw the Washburn campus.

Among those he called on was Zenas Crane of Dalton, Mas-

The class of 1902, sitting for its group portrait the same year that the campus building behind them was renamed Rice Hall.

Norman Plass

Ceremonial arch built for Plass' inauguration.

sachusetts, the wealthy and philanthropic grandson of the founder of a paper company. Crane contributed to colleges and had backed Admiral Robert Peary's expedition to the North Pole.

Crane also dabbled in astronomy, and Plass persuaded him to give Washburn a building and equipment to study the stars — including a sophisticated telescope. The gift would total $56,000. Also, there would be funds for the study of physics and mathematics. In return, Crane asked that his name be kept secret as long as he lived.

The college and Topeka soon were "electrified" with news of this large but anonymous contribution. The announcement was made to the students by Professor D. M. Fisk in a chapel session. Fisk credited it to the work of Field Secretary Plass.

In reporting the gift the editors of *The Washburn Review* conceded that "we had heard, rather vaguely of Mr. Plass, our financial agent in the East." Concluding, they wrote, "It seems after long years of slow, steady, substantial growth of Washburn the time has come for rapid fruition." Indeed, the time had come.

First, however, there was the matter of finding a new president to replace George Herrick. In October 1901 the trustees offered the post to George August Gates, until recently the president of Iowa College, a Congregationalist school in Grinnell, Iowa. But Gates and his wife, finding the Kansas climate not to their liking, turned Washburn down.

That shifted the trustees' attention to their highly effective field secretary. Plass was a New York native with a divinity degree from Yale, and an ordained Congregational minister. He had been pastor of churches in the East and Midwest and superintendent of the Anti-Saloon League in Rhode Island and New York. He fit the bill.

The 42-year-old Plass was elected to the presidency on June 10, 1902. At his inauguration in October, a triumphal arch led to the chapel, where blue bunting decked the place and hundreds of blue flags flew. Students wore buttons bearing Plass' likeness.

He did not disappoint his employers or his colleagues. Over the next six years, enrollment in college-level courses would more than double. So would Washburn's annual budget. The faculty would quadruple in size. The campus would blossom with new structures.

Zenas Crane

The anonymous observatory opened in 1903, the same year as a new president's home, which the Plass family was the first to occupy. Along the way came a heating plant that provided steam for all campus structures.

In 1904, the fortune of industrialist Andrew Carnegie delivered $40,000 to Washburn for a new library. When it opened in June 1905, the Carnegie building replaced Boswell Hall as home of the book collection. Shortly afterward there opened new engineering shops and then a gymnasium, begun in 1908 and supported by a $43,000 donation from Washburn Trustee Jonathan Thomas. It was named as a memorial to his late son, Charles Brooks Thomas.

The endowment — one of the keys to

"It seems after long years of slow, steady, substantial growth of Washburn the time has come for rapid fruition."

– *Washburn Review*

A secret "cornerstone"

The man who designed and built the new observatory evidently was paid for his work, but clearly he felt cheated out of the credits.

So L.M. Wood and others who constructed the building fashioned their own copper box, filled it with memorabilia and stashed it inside a wall — all unbeknownst to the college officials, who had produced their own cornerstone time capsule.

In Wood's box, he enclosed a letter giving reasons for the covert action:

"All over the country it is customary for those in charge to mention the name of the architect of the building, together with those of the contactors" when a cornerstone is filled. Not so at the Washburn Observatory.

"They did not forget," the architect continued, "to laud some of the old members of the board of trustees, who, while they had their value in the early days of the college, should have resigned twenty years ago...."

As a result, "We, that is myself and the contactors, concluded that we would have a copper box of our own."

The Observatory in a tinted postcard, circa 1910; the disgruntled architect, L.M. Wood, left.

Wood added some thoughts about the Prohibition movement — "The people of Kansas do not want to enforce it so much as they want to talk about doing it" — along with estimates of the number of saloons, houses of prostitution and gambling outfits still operating in the state.

His letter foresaw the time when his secret "cornerstone" box would be uncovered — "perhaps a hundred years from now, when the building is torn down." Only 60-odd years would elapse, however, before the tornado of 1966 ripped apart the building. Inside, workers found Wood's copper box. Besides Wood's letter it contained photographs of himself, sheet music he wrote and an array of other items from 1903 —theater tickets, souvenirs and cartoons.

making Plass' "business" go — expanded by at least one-third. In 1905, Washburn's 40th anniversary, Plass kicked off a campaign aimed at garnering $1 million over 10 years. By 1907, Plass reported, the campaign had already gathered $325,000 in pledges and soon would reach $350,000.

Plass also worked deals with Topekans to whom the college owed money, transferring to them college-owned Topeka lots, most of them residential, in return for canceling $190,000 in debts.

After two years of watching the boom go on around them, the editors of the new *Kaw* yearbook were agog at Washburn's "accelerated evolution."

"With no minimizing of the great record of 39 years," the yearbook's opening essay said, "the college has never before known a like period of vivid life, progress, surprises or

A panoramic camera captured central campus about 1910. The view is to the south, stretching from east on the left to west on the right. The structures, from left: MacVicar Chapel, Rice Hall, Carnegie Library, Thomas Gymnasium and Boswell Hall.

1902-1918

1902: On May 13, the chapel was named for Washburn's longtime president, Peter McVicar. The first building constructed on the 160-acre campus — known as Main or Science hall — was renamed for one of the founders, Harvey Rice. Both men attended the dedication ceremony.
1903: The observatory, donated anonymously by Zenas Crane, was opened.
— On June 5, former President McVicar died. On June 11, early Washburn proponent and longtime trustee Rice died.
— A new home for the president was constructed. It would be called "The White House."
1904: The *Kaw* yearbook published its first issue. Unlike *Helianthus*, which lasted only a few years in the mid-1890s, the *Kaw* survived.
1905: Blue was officially chosen as the color of Washburn, inspired by Yale's school color.
— Carnegie Library, begun in 1904, was dedicated in 1905.
— Washburn men organized a basketball team, which won nine games and lost four in its first season, 1905-1906.
1907: Rice Hall burned on December 6, probably the result of a repairman's accident. The top two floors were destroyed, and Rice was rebuilt minus its bell tower.
1908: Frank Sanders inaugurated president.
1909: Thomas Gymnasium dedicated.
1911: President William Howard Taft, on a tour of Midwestern states, visited the Washburn campus.
1912: Student Council was organized.
— Sagamore men's honorary society began.
1913: The Medical School, which had struggled to meet rising standards for medical education since its beginning, merged with the University of Kansas Medical School.
1915: Washburn celebrated its 50th anniversary during commencement week.
— Parley Womer was elected the sixth president of Washburn, also during commencement week.
1916: On November 10 — one day before a big football game against KU — students dressed in raggedy clothes as part of the first Hobo Day.
1917: With U.S. entry into the Great War

in Europe, classes were shortened and activities altered to prepare students for wartime service.

— The senior women's honorary society, Nonoso, was organized. The name came from the first letters of Washburn's motto: *Non Nobis Solum*, "Not for ourselves alone".

1918: The death of Zenas Crane allowed the college to name the building after him.

— The Law School moved from downtown Topeka to the Washburn campus, mostly so students could participate in Student Army Training Corps activities. The school was quartered in Crane Observatory.

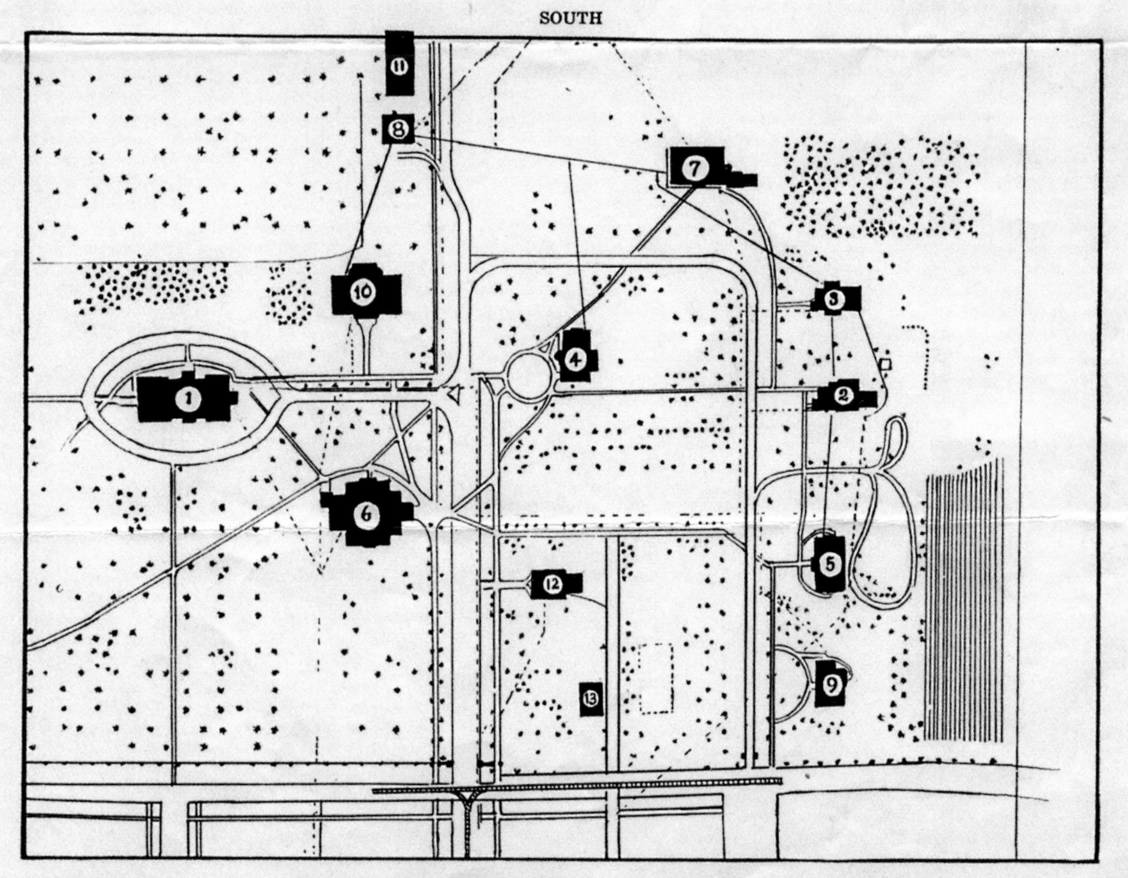

Campus map of 1907.

Washburn Orchestra, 1904.

Symbol of the saloon smasher, mailed to Norman Plass from Carrie Nation's Topeka jail cell. The note said, "If any man suffer as a Christian let him not be ashamed but let him glorify God on this behalf."

promise."

The Washburn Review declared Plass "an idol with the student body."

Diversions — proper ones

Vigorous as he was in pushing the college into the energetic new century, Plass maintained the conservative orderliness still expected in a religious-founded institution. He opposed student dancing and card-playing at general student functions, and these positions were applauded by alumni and other Topekans.

No less a temperance crusader than Carrie Nation wrote him from a jail cell in Topeka on December 13, 1902, where she was serving a 10-day term for disturbing the peace. She had visited a Topeka drugstore, suspecting it sold liquor on the sly, and tried to force her way past the proprietor. Police arrived and arrested her. In her note to Plass, she enclosed a hatchet pin, symbolic of her crusade against saloons. No doubt, she was impressed by Plass' experience as head of Anti-Saloon leagues in Rhode Island and New York and she commended his strict rules for students.

Washburn Campus and Field, a publication for alumni, vigorously denied reports that "staid old Washburn" planned to give a "swell dance." That Washburn had ever staged anything of the sort, the publication maintained, was a "groundless assertion."

Perhaps too many Washburn students had too little time for high living. *Campus and Field* reported the results of a survey of male students, in which three in ten said they paid all their expenses through their own earnings. Another three in ten earned the money for the majority of their expenses.

Literary societies continued into the new century, aimed, according to the *Kaw*, at preparing women and men for "public life." They trained their members in public speaking, both prepared and extemporaneous, and debate. A dramatic club supported those with a theatrical bent. Also introduced was the first honor society, Tau Delta Pi.

Not all pursuits were serious, however. In 1903 the college dropped its ban on social fraternities and sororities, and three popped up right away. All were local groups, beginning with Sigma Delta Psi sorority, Beta sorority and Delta Phi fraternity. Eventually, each affiliated with a national body: respectively Kappa Alpha Theta, Alpha Phi and Phi Delta Theta. Others were formed as the century unfolded.

Students were allowed, for the first time, to attend performances at theaters in town. And in 1905 the roller skating fad swept the campus.

Football grew in popularity. For a few years, girls' basketball prospered, but in 1906 travel to play other Kansas teams was prohibited and the team disbanded.

New avenues of learning

As the new century dawned, Washburn had three divisions — a College of Arts and Sciences, a Department of Music and Art, and the Academy to get high-school-age youth ready for college.

Plass meant to make Washburn more like a university than a college, and in his tenure the college began a concerted program of academic growth.

First the music and art departments were combined with the oratory program. Into this was blended a separate downtown Topeka art school, the Reid-Stone School. The combination emerged as the Washburn School of Fine Arts.

Law School

Washburn's new Law School opened in September 1903 with a three-year course of study leading to a bachelor of laws degree. Entrants had to have a high-school education or the equivalent. Washburn College offered a combined six-year program leading to bachelor's degrees in liberal arts and law.

Law classes met in rented rooms on the third floor of a building at 118 W. Eighth Avenue in downtown Topeka. The college promoted the site as being near all courts — federal, state and local — for the practical benefit of student observation. Topeka lawyers pitched in, one donating his entire law library and others volunteering to teach.

In 1911, the Law School moved to 725-727 Kansas Avenue and in 1913 to another downtown site, a building vacated by Bell Telephone at 211 W. Sixth Avenue.

In 1918, by which time law enrollment had surpassed 80, the entrance requirement was raised to a year of college. That same year, the school moved to Crane Observatory on the Washburn campus so law students could participate in the Student Army Training Corps.

All around the town: Washburn Law's first three buildings: Top, 118 W. Eighth; middle, 725 Kansas Avenue; bottom, 211 W. Sixth with freshman class posing outside.

Then came the merger with the Kansas Medical College, founded in 1889 by Topeka doctors. At the time, the Medical School had 100 students; classes were held at 12th and Tyler streets in Topeka.

And in 1903 Washburn started its own Law School, a project of Topeka lawyers at the urging of Plass. In its first year the Law School had 41 students and a Harvard graduate, Ernest B. Conant, as dean. It, too, operated from a building in downtown Topeka to be near courts and the Capitol.

Eventually, an engineering program was established along with one in theology. The latter was the dream of a Topeka businessman who had donated money "to fill a need for more Bible instruction for all students."

Plass even dreamed of starting a dental school, but that never came to pass.

He also strove to modernize existing course offerings. To the traditional Latin — which had outstripped Greek in favor — he added a requirement to take a modern foreign language such as French or Spanish.

Faculty, which numbered 23 in 1901, grew to 112 by 1908. In 1901, students in college-level courses totaled about 300. By 1908, college-level enrollment had surpassed 700.

Plass boasted that Washburn outstripped every other college competitor in Kansas — thus not including the university in Lawrence — in size of teaching force, in value, number and quality of buildings, and in equipment.

Through all this, Washburn's budget ballooned from about $29,500 in the 1901-1902 academic year to nearly $75,000 in 1907-1908.

Despite Plass' promotional skill, however, and perhaps because of booming enrollment and campus growth, Washburn's income did not rise as fast as its expenses. The average student paid $40 in tuition but cost the college $95.

Moving on

Plass' star burned brightly — the *Kaw* yearbook called his work "stupendous" — but, as Washburn presidential terms go, only briefly. In summer 1907, while he still was president of Washburn, Plass organized the Norman Plass Lumber Company with himself

The red stone wall

Each year in the early 1900s, the college Dramatic Club donated money raised by its plays for use on campus. In 1906, the club's gift paid for a stone gate and wall, built of native red boulders and mortar at the College Avenue entrance off 17th Street. Funds came from proceeds of "Woodbarrow Farm," a comedy produced by the club at the Grand Opera House downtown.

The gate took the form of an entryway bounded by six-foot stone pillars and and a low stone wall. Through the 1910s the club, along with faculty members and various graduating classes, came up with more money to extend the wall and add more gates.

In announcing the gift of the Class of 1915, *The Review* opined that campus beautification "ought to be in the hands of the student body and this is where each one should do his part."

By the early 1920s, the red stone wall and gates reached east to Mulvane Street and west to Jewell Avenue.

Stone gate at College Avenue entrance, the work of the Dramatic Club.

Hitting the books in the reading room of Carnegie Library. Its exterior appeared in a tinted postcard, above right.

as president. The firm, shares of which he sold to Topeka businessmen, marketed timber from forests in British Columbia.

In September 1907, Plass told the executive committee of the trustees that the new business would make him "too busy to devote full time to Washburn College," and announced he would leave as of June 1908.

After he left Washburn, Plass' venture into private business foundered when he became head of a Boston company that offered to invest the money of busy professionals. U.S. postal officials closed the company amid complaints that it had nothing near the resources it claimed. Plass and two other officers pleaded guilty in 1910 to mail fraud and paid fines.

By then, Washburn had a new president, who was two years into his term. In April 1908, the trustees chose a recognized religious scholar, Frank Sanders. In selecting him, they sought to consolidate the gains of the century's first decade and to burnish Washburn's academic standing. For 19 years Sanders had taught at Yale and also been dean of its school of religion. He was an ordained Congregationalist minister. Sanders, whose parents were American missionaries, was born on the island of Ceylon, now Sri Lanka. Sanders had taught in India for several years, and also published multiple respected volumes on religious history. Well-established publishers sought him out to write works of theology.

In his inaugural address, Sanders foresaw Washburn's enrollment rising to 1,500 or even 1,800 and maintaining itself as an institution of "like grade" with KU. But to carry out his plan, there would need to be more faculty with better pay and shorter hours. More dormitories would be needed because, he said, the college's "best work will not be done until a larger proportion of students lives on campus."

The greatest need, Sanders said, would be

Frank Sanders

to achieve the million-dollar endowment for which Plass had campaigned, and the greatest push would have to be among Kansans.

In an editorial, *The Topeka Daily Capital* called Sanders "the right man in the right place."

Not what the job seemed

When Sanders came to Washburn to interview for the presidency, he was told by Plass, a couple of trustees and the treasurer that the campaign for the endowment would reach $350,000 within months.

The facts were otherwise. Upon taking office, Sanders found that the campaign had fallen short of that mark by $150,000. Charitably, Sanders blamed Plass only for being over-optimistic, but he complained that the effect was to deceive him about the status of the place where he was taking a position.

Among the donors who had come up with money, Sanders found, there was dismay that fundraisers were still knocking on their doors.

A considerable number of donors, it turned out, simply had not fulfilled their pledges. Among the donors who had come up with money, Sanders found, there was dismay that fundraisers were still knocking on their doors. Hadn't Norman Plass promised them a five-year moratorium on requests? That too, came as a surprise.

Sanders also was led to believe that the college was operating in the black, but he soon found an operating deficit of at least $10,000.

Vice President Hiram B. Harrison, brought on board to help with fundraising.

In his first report to the trustees, Sanders graciously complimented Plass for his efforts. His predecessor, Sanders said, had carried the college "nearly through the period of rapid development from a small college to a university." Yet with the discoveries about the true state of the fundraising campaigns, the endowment and the deficit, Sanders told the trustees that the college was "almost at a standstill." And Washburn, he pointed out, had borrowed to its limits.

To Sanders, raising money was distasteful. In 1909, his second year on the job, he proposed that the trustees create the new position of vice president to ply potential donors for money. In June 1910, the trustees agreed and Hiram B. Harrison was hired for the post.

Harrison found plenty to worry about. By January 1912, he was sounding dire warnings about Washburn's finances.

"For twenty years," Harrison wrote the trustees, "the college has drawn largely on land sales, and the land is now gone." How would it overcome operating deficits? One method was to mortgage part of the 160-acre campus, which it proceeded to do, to pay off part of its debt and meet its current bills.

"May we have wisdom more than human to meet the difficulties before us," Harrison said, adding that all efforts should be placed into a fundraising campaign.

Unhappily for Sanders and for the college, Harrison was better at calling on others to make greater effort than at giving it himself. Sanders confided that Harrison was "a bit of an egotist" who complained about salary and vacations but showed few immediate results. The vice president, because of unspecified "larger ambitions," in Sanders' words, did not devote his "full energy" to raising money and Washburn's problems remained.

Money problems aside, Sanders' strength lay in the educational function of the college and he was thought to have improved matters there, boosting the quality of Washburn's program. He brought it favorable repute among educators and, more importantly, potential students.

The college life: Students tasted the spread at an indoor picnic in 1910. Did the umbrella symbolize a retreat from a rainy day outdoors?

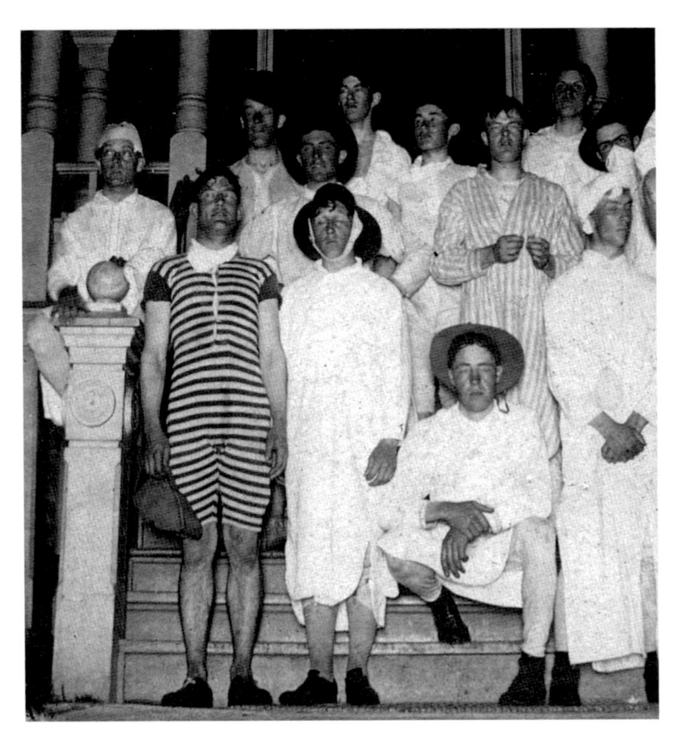

Turn-of-the-century sights: Students, mules and a stack of hay on campus in 1906, above. Left: Nightshirt parade brought a delegation of men to the steps of Holbrook Hall, a women's dormitory, in 1903.

Daniel Moses Fisk began Washburn's sociology program, the second in the country, in 1899. He taught at the college until 1924 and was one of Washburn's leading promoters in the early 20th century. His classroom in the basement of Carnegie contained its own sociology library.

Averse as he was to beating the bushes for contributions, Sanders evidently felt at ease marketing his college to the youth of Kansas. In 1910, he distributed circulars mentioning Washburn's "moral and religious influences" to appeal to youth — and not coincidentally their parents. He also sought support from teachers in and outside of Kansas, and from alumni, and placed recruitment advertisements in out-of-town newspapers such as *The Kansas City Star* and *The Kansas City Journal.*

Sanders rejected complaints that he was trying to intrude on the efforts of Baker, the Methodist college in Baldwin City, and other religious-based colleges. Washburn, he wrote one Methodist minister, simply was trying to lure those who might otherwise enroll at KU or K-State.

Sanders also began the college's first full-fledged summer school, which in 1910 drew 56 students.

All around the campus

In his first year in office, Sanders envisioned a student-led effort to improve the campus. It would be called the Campus Improvement Association and its first efforts would be to remodel athletic fields, pave sidewalks and generally spruce up the place. Later, the association would take on the job of improving streets. Sanders proposed the idea to students at the regular chapel gathering on May 21, 1908. Four days later, at the session ending the academic year, the association was approved. Graduating seniors pledged $500 to the effort.

The work could be messy: One of the tasks was to remove bagworm webs from cedar and pine trees, and the students collected six bushels of the stuff.

Another campus improvement came from the local electric utility. Sanders persuaded it to place two bright streetlights on campus — one at the library and one at Hartford Cottage — to relieve anxiety felt by "unescorted women." Washburn, Sanders said, was used as a public park, and sometimes by unsavory types. Unlighted stretches of

How the school year was scheduled

Through all of Washburn's expansion in the early 1900s, the basic fact of college life remained attending classes, and the school year began later than it would in the 21st century.

The first semester started well into September and rolled over into the next calendar year.

The 1906 *Bulletin* listed registration on September 11 and the first day of classes September 12. The first break was for Thanksgiving. Classes were dismissed just before noon on Wednesday, November 28, the eve of the holiday, and resumed the next Monday, December 3. The Christmas recess began December 21 and ended January 8. Then the first semester resumed, not ending until January 29.

The second semester began January 30, breaking for Washington's Birthday on February 22 and for May Day. Commencement took place in early June.

With the biggest banner of all, the Washburn chapter stood out at a 1909 YWCA college conference in Colorado.

campus amounted to "an invitation to those who are looking for…retreats where they will be hidden from inspection."

Protecting women was the tenor of the times on campuses. At a conference of Midwest colleges in 1911, discussion centered on co-education. Girls and boys, participants stated, must be handled differently. Girls could not be allowed many liberties, requiring supervision at dances and even picnics.

For the minority of women students who lived in dormitories on campus, Washburn's rules called for absolute quiet from 10 p.m. to 6:45 a.m. weekdays and from 3:30 to 4:30 p.m. on Sundays. No baths were allowed from 10 p.m. to 6 a.m.

Girls were not allowed to attend parties on school nights, with an occasional exception for seniors. They must depart the parties by 11 p.m.

Sanders maintained many of the strict social rules, including supervision of both sexes at various events.

Still, some students pushed the envelope, notably a group calling itself the Xystos Club. Despite faculty disapproval, the club held a dance in December 1912. As a result, it was denied recognition and its leaders were banned from classes until they promised to conform to the rules.

But Sanders' administration occasionally practiced a kind of college democracy. In 1912, the matter of holidays was put to the students: should Washburn take a holiday for Easter, extending from the Thursday before through the Monday after the day itself, in exchange for its existing holidays on Washington's Birthday and May Day?

Yes! the students said, in a nearly unanimous response. The faculty agreed and so a new holiday schedule came into being.

For a church-founded institution, Washburn did not heavily emphasize religion — at least by the standards of the day, when

The 1904 womens' basketball team played Baker, Haskell, Topeka YWCA and Topeka High School.

Sports: "We have won the game and nothing else matters."

On college campuses across America, the 1900s brought a surge in the popularity of football — a rough and sometimes bloody sport for the players and an alternately exhilarating and depressing one for spectators.

Washburn had fielded teams through the 1890s and seemed to have mastered the sport a few years into the new century. In 1903, the Washburn eleven won seven games, lost none and tied only one. The next two years brought more seven-victory seasons, all marked by the crushing kind of runs into the middle of the line that represented the standard of football in that day. Because of injuries, in some quarters pressure built to abolish the sport. Its proponents suggested instead that new rules were in order.

After the end of the 1905 football season — a particularly brutal one marked by injuries and deaths in other parts of the country — Washburn played one additional contest, a "clinical" test of new rules.

On Christmas Day 1905, the Washburn team traveled to Wichita to play the team from Fairmount College under new rules purportedly designed to make the game safer. Part of the experiment was to allow the ball to be passed from behind the line of scrimmage to a teammate downfield. Also among the proposed rules: players who slugged other players would be disqualified, and the offensive team would lose possession if it committed any foul.

Washburn's short-lived rowing team, as depicted in the 1908 Kaw. *It would reappear as a club in 1969.*

In the contest that day, several passes were, indeed, thrown, but with none of the precision that would become common decades later. Players tossed the egg-shaped ball with both hands, much the way they might have passed a basketball. Several passes were completed, but not enough to give either team an advantage. Kicking and running wound up about equal, and the game ended in a scoreless tie.

The next year, college football across America allowed use of the forward pass to advance the ball.

The 1907 Washburn football squad, coached by Garfield Weede, went undefeated and, like the 1903 team, won the Kansas Conference championship. Among its conquests were the University of Kansas, Kansas State and the University of Oklahoma.

The KU game, played Saturday, November 2, at Washburn drew an estimated 4,500 spectators. Both teams used the forward pass. Washburn threw the ball 10 times and completed five passes. KU tried five and completed three. Washburn won, 12-5.

Two days later, students discovered signs saying "No school today," in celebration of the victory. A chapel session turned into a celebration.

Players who slugged other players would be disqualified and the offensive team would lose possession if it committed any foul.

Above: Washburn vs. Oklahoma, 1907. Left: Promoting the big game with KU, early 1900s.

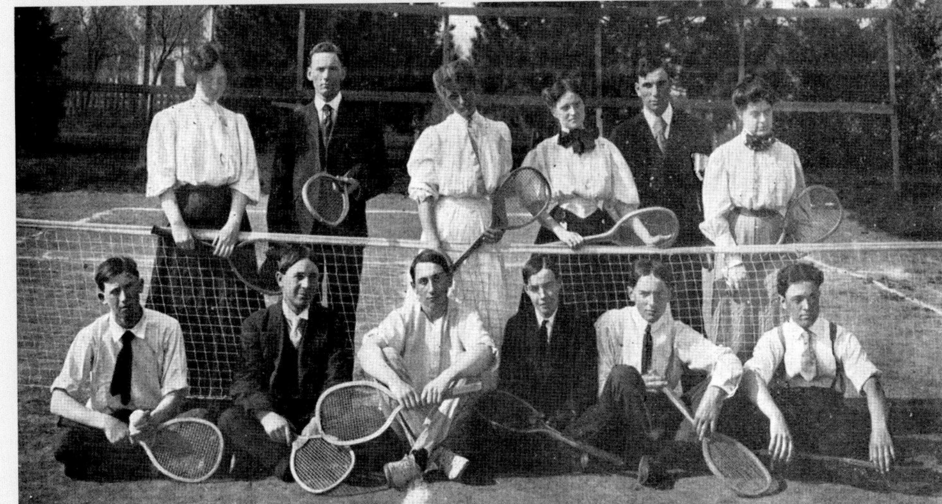

Above, tennis club in 1906. Left, the 1904 track team, with a trophy.

Coach, captain and team members were cheered. One of the Washburn players, Bottles Hope, responded to cries for speeches: "Well, I don't know what I've got to say except I'm glad we kind of took 'em. That's all."

Dean McEachron summed up the feeling: "We have won the game and nothing else matters."

Students, administrators and the football team then paraded into downtown Topeka. At the Capitol, they received congratulations from the governor.

Washburn would beat the Jayhawks only one more time, in 1912. The teams last played in 1945.

Women formed Washburn's first basketball team, which prospered for a few years after the turn of the century. The Washburn team crowned itself champions of Kansas after beating Haskell Institute in 1904. In 1906, however, the faculty voted to ban travel to out-of-town games and the women's team was disbanded.

In late 1905, a men's basketball team was formed under coach Harry C. Byrd and won the conference championship four years later.

Eligibility problems cropped up frequently — and sometimes embarrassingly — in early 20th-century college sports. In 1909, the Washburn baseball team tried to skirt the rules, using a couple of ineligible players in games at St. Mary's and Manhattan. Coaches defended themselves by saying they needed the extra players to fill out the team; otherwise, they could not have played the games. The problem of using an ineligible player occurred again in 1911 and this time the manager and captain were deposed and the season ended.

Not long after the latter incident, the faculty adopted rules for participation in athletics — and also in debate, dramatics and oratory. The rules required participants to be enrolled in at least 12 credit hours in courses leading to a degree.

The medics and their home: Above, sophomore class of medical students, 1911. Right, Kansas Medical College's one-time building at 5th & Quincy. The school was part of Washburn from 1902 to 1913.

Charlotte Mendell Leavitt joined the Washburn faculty in 1899 and taught for 41 years. During her tenure she also served as dean of women and as head of the English department. She suggested a motto for Washburn that remains today: "Non nobis solum," Not for ourselves alone.

many Americans considered religion an important part of mainstream life. The regular "chapel" services served essentially as student-faculty-administration meetings, and only the monthly vespers services qualified as religious activities under the college's auspices. Sanders considered the religious preferences of the students widely distributed, although by that he meant distributed among five Christian denominations. At his inauguration, Sanders had said, "Proud as Washburn ever will be of its Puritan heritage and ready to acknowledge its fealty, it will never be managed for denominational ends."

The Young Men's and Young Women's Christian Associations — YMCA and YWCA — were active on campus. They were formed in 1900 and 1901 from earlier Christian groups.

Medical troubles

Meanwhile, the medical college proved to be an incurable headache, and money lay at the root of the problem. A Carnegie Foundation representative who examined the department, its instructional staff and equipment, said in early 1910 that it was failing the grade on all fronts. Any hope for supporting the medical college was beyond the reach of Washburn and its "weak endowment," his report said. Sanders acknowledged that the medical department was "fighting for its life."

Representatives of the American Medical Association reduced the school's rating from "A" to "B," which meant it needed improving or it might lose AMA accreditation and its graduates would be unable to practice in many states. AMA complaints about the school included poor organization, insufficient equipment and disconnection from the rest of the college whose name it bore. At the time of the merger in 1903, the Medical School administrators had been promised quasi-independent status.

Sanders proposed to strengthen the college administration's role in selection of faculty, and to eliminate the faculty's right to name a representative to the Board of Trustees. The alternative, Sanders believed, was "extinction."

In 1910 oversight was reorganized. With donations of equipment and money from Topeka doctors, the school won a brief reprieve. But in early 1911, the Carnegie Foundation's president urged Sanders to give up the battle and merge the medical unit with the University of Kansas' Medical School in the Kansas City metropolitan area. KU, he said, could draw a stronger medical faculty because "young men with the best training will gravitate to large centers of business and population" — in this case, Kansas City.

In 1912 the AMA lowered its rating of Washburn's Medical School all the way to "C," meaning that in many states Washburn medical graduates would not be able to practice.

The next year, Washburn pulled the plug and merged the medical school with KU's. In

June that year, KU Chancellor Frank Strong asked the state Board of Regents to approve the merger, and it was done.

The merger was a tough pill to swallow because KU was never far from the minds of Washburn administrators. The university down the Kansas River was constantly growing and, in Washburn's view, competing for its students and its territory. Sanders described to the trustees "the ever-increasing pressure of the State University, even in our own fields."

For its part, he said, Washburn was not trying to rival KU. Instead, its aim was to develop a "distinctively Christian institution of the higher class."

Still a money problem

In June 1910, a committee of the trustees recommended yet more fundraising and also cuts in spending. Sanders suggested tapping endowment funds to pay off debt, which the trustees' finance committee refused to do. In a pointed reply to Sanders' idea the trustees' secretary, L.H. Greenwood, advised Sanders that the time was ripe for raising money from Topekans and also for saving it.

"There ought to be new energy expended toward raising money," he wrote Sanders,

The only President of the United States who visited Washburn while in office, William Howard Taft, left of flag, dedicated a flagpole honoring Civil War veterans. The ceremony took place outside Thomas Gymnasium on September 27, 1911.

Social reformer and friend of the college

A minister with a literary bent and a reformist temperament, Charles Monroe Sheldon arrived in Topeka from New England in 1888. He was 31 years old and full of ideas and energy. As a Congregationalist, he naturally gravitated toward Congregationalist-founded Washburn, serving as a trustee in the 1910s and as a frequent speaker and motivator for the college and its students.

Charles Sheldon

Central Congregational Church hired Sheldon as pastor. Quickly, he developed a following with a series of Sunday-evening sermons based on real life and delivered with cliffhanger endings. Members of the congregation learned the resolution of his stories only if they returned the next week. The sermons were devised to appeal to young people and, in particular, Washburn College students, whom he saw as future civic leaders.

The late 19th century was marked in Christian religious circles by the Social Gospel movement, which set itself the goal of helping the poor. Sheldon persuaded members of his church to figure out what they could do for impoverished black families who lived in a neighborhood called Tennessee Town, not far from the church building. He inspired the establishment of a kindergarten for African-American children in 1893, the first kindergarten of any kind in Topeka.

Sheldon gained his greatest fame as the author of a book, *In His Steps*, published in 1897, which drew from his sermons. Millions of copies have been sold worldwide since, and its memorable subtitle, "What would Jesus Do?" remains a popular phrase among some Christians in the 21st century. In 1900, the publisher of *The Topeka Daily Capital* turned the newspaper over to him for a week, letting Sheldon edit it the way he thought Jesus Christ might have. Sheldon chose mainly good news.

Sheldon also campaigned for equality among races and sexes, for prohibition and against war. He died in Topeka in 1946.

Time for recreation and rah-rah: A class picnic in 1910, above. Below left, men's dormitory room adorned with team pennants and posters. Below right, the rooters club in 1917.

Below: in June 1915 Washburn marked its 50th anniversary with speeches, receptions, banquets and a historical pageant for the college and the community. Re-enacting the conflicts of territorial days were members of the Women's Federation of Topeka. Various clubs in Topeka contributed to the celebration in addition to students and faculty.

"and less toward spending it."

By March 1911, the trustees even contemplated selling off lots from the eastern edge of the 160-acre campus to raise funds. Stiff opposition from alumni and students quashed that idea.

Sanders cautioned the faculty about becoming too harsh with poor students. Otherwise, Washburn might lose their tuition money.

"Patience and friendliness," he counseled in a letter, would retain students. "Those we have a chance to become loyal and efficient graduates."

The money crisis went on and on, and President Sanders felt ill-equipped to handle it. He was no fundraiser, he continued to say, and had not been hired to be one.

As for the Congregationalists, of the denomination that brought Washburn into being only one Kansas congregation donated anything — Topeka's Central Congregational. Other than that, Sanders reported in 1910, "not one Kansas church sends a dollar to Washburn."

Campus and Field complimented individual New England Congregationalists for their support — $7 for every $1 raised from individuals in Kansas. In the same breath it asked, "What is Congregationalist Kansas doing?"

"The fact is," according to the alumni newsletter, "New England has not yet weaned her 'Pioneer Kansas' child."

Sanders compared his situation to the years of Peter McVicar's presidency, an era still fondly recalled in the institutional memory of Washburn. Sanders minimized it as a gentler, simpler time when problems were minor and standards lower. Nowadays, the president said, Washburn had all the complexity of a small university.

Adding to Sanders' troubles, the attempt to turn fundraising over to a vice-president failed. In June 1912, Hiram Harrison was let go; he moved to a pastorate in Kansas City,

The bell

When Washburn opened for classes on its new campus in 1874, the main building had no belfry. That changed in 1880, when Charles Boswell, the prominent New England donor, gave a bell to the college. A belfry was added to receive it.

Mounted in the belfry, the bell rang the hour and times for church services and afternoon study hours. Also, it rang tidings of Washburn victories in football, baseball, oratory and debate. A later president called it "traditionally Washburn's most precious possession."

For students, the bell was also a temptation to make noise on Halloween. Sometimes its clapper disappeared and the bell was otherwise occasionally mistreated.

Sometimes, it was simply overused. On October 27, 1906, after Washburn beat Kansas State Agricultural College, 5-4, in football, exuberant ringers cracked it with a sledge hammer. The next year, fire broke out in the upper floors of Rice Hall, destroying the belfry. The bell dropped to the second floor and was found under the debris. What now?

In 1910 the bell was placed briefly on the library lawn and the graduating class of that year donated $500 to have it mounted permanently. In late November 1910, no site having been determined, six members of the 1911 graduating class removed the bell and stashed it off campus. At the 1911 commencement, under cover of night, a concrete foundation was laid and covered with sod. Not long afterward, masons built a pedestal for the bell and the object was welcomed back with a ceremony.

Only days later, the bell disappeared again, and rumors flew that this was the work of the class of 1910, unhappy that the 1911 class had stolen its glory. The bell went missing for three years, until commencement 1914, when the graduating class of that year found the bell in a small cave on property belonging to the family of a 1910 graduate. Members returned it to campus on a wagon surrounded by a procession of graduates.

Bell mounted near Rice Hall, about 1916.

Parley Womer

Missouri.

In November 1912, four and one-half years after he accepted the job as Washburn president, Frank Sanders submitted his resignation. His letter to the trustees said he believed he had "lost the cooperation of the trustees as a body." The public announcement mentioned differences between the trustees and Sanders over "methods of raising money," which presumably referred to the expectation that the president of the college ought to take a leading role. Years later, Sanders' daughter and, separately, the college librarian in a remembrance, cited additional differences between Sanders and the trustees over educational matters. Sanders, they said, had proved too liberal for some of the conservative trustees.

To the trustees, Sanders wrote that he understood he had been accused of neglecting Washburn's affairs in favor of outside interests — probably referring to his many invitations to appear before college and church associations.

Nevertheless, the student-edited *Review* praised his tenure.

"Dr. Sanders represents the highest type of ideals," the student newspaper said. "We believe... that President Sanders has raised the moral and ideal tone of the college. He has been a leader around whom the students were glad to rally."

The resignation was to have taken effect on July 1, 1913. One month beforehand, the trustees asked him to withdraw the resignation and instead to take an indefinite leave of absence. Sanders would spend that time trying to raise money from foundations and individuals in the East. Retaining the title of president, it was thought, would give him more authority in asking for money.

Sanders had made no secret of his aversion to fundraising, yet he did find money in the East. He persuaded the General Education Board to put up funds if the college came up with a greater amount.

In September 1914, Sanders — who by then was working in New York City — submitted his second and final resignation. He went to work for the Board of Missionary Preparation, which set standards for people departing for other continents to serve as religious missionaries.

Duncan McEachron, dean of the college of liberal arts, was named vice president in June 1913. He would manage the affairs of Washburn until the arrival of a new president.

A new head man, and a money raiser

On June 8, 1915, the trustees elected Parley Womer, pastor of a church in St. Paul, Minnesota, to become Washburn's president. He took office September 1.

The 45-year-old Womer was a striking individual. A tall, fit and eagle-eyed Vermont native who favored high, starched collars, one observer said Womer "would be noticed in any crowd." Womer led the college through a World War, the high expectations of the Roaring 20s and a tempestuous battle with a professor over faculty rights.

When he took office, Womer would say later, he found Washburn burdened with a "huge debt," an inadequate endowment, dilapidated buildings and "pitifully small" faculty salaries.

He went to work to turn that around, and to a large extent he succeeded.

By June 1917, Washburn's endowment reached $500,000, short of Norman Plass' long-ago goal of $1 million but nevertheless a milestone in the life of the college. *The Review* thanked in particular the people of Topeka, a constituency that previous administrations had long wished would come forth. The enlarged endowment seemed to portend an end to the days of annual deficits.

Womer was awash in praise from his employers — the trustees. They called him a "tireless, constant and undiscouraged worker.

He is a real president."

And Womer was not done trying to right the ship.

An electric streetcar approached the Washburn stone gate at College Avenue in the early 20th century.

Thoroughly collegiate

For much of Washburn's history, the Academy or preparatory department had played a large role in the life of the institution. After the Civil War, high schools were few in Kansas and from its beginning Washburn faced the need to prepare youth even to begin collegiate-level work. Unlike some public schools, however, it did not see itself as a holding pen.

"The Academy is not a school for boys and girls needing restraint," the 1907 *Bulletin* said, "but rather for young men and women who have sufficient maturity to appreciate the advantages offered them. Students whose examples or influence are injurious...are asked to withdraw."

Even late in the 19th century, the Academy provided the bulk of the institution's enrollment. But after the turn of the century, with the growth of public secondary education in Kansas, administrators saw a decline in Academy numbers. In 1916-1917 enrollment dropped below 70. In 1917-1918, it declined to 37. Tuitions brought in $900 and expenses totaled $3,500, a drain on Washburn resources. That reversed the situation of the early years, when only the preparatory department paid its way.

It was time, President Womer told the Board of Trustees, for Washburn to unburden itself of the Academy. It could be turned over to adjacent, rural school districts — Washburn

The college Shakespeare Club in 1905.

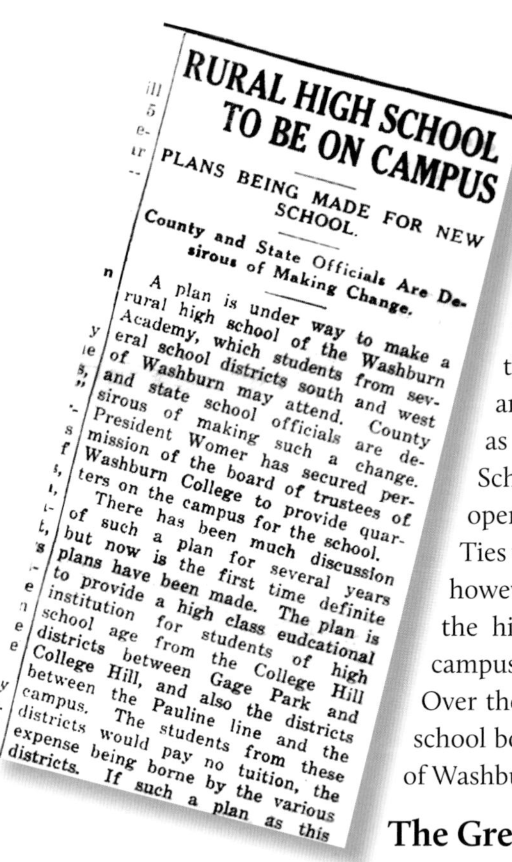
RURAL HIGH SCHOOL TO BE ON CAMPUS

PLANS BEING MADE FOR NEW SCHOOL.

County and State Officials Are Desirous of Making Change.

A plan is under way to make a rural high school of the Washburn Academy, which students from several school districts south and west of Washburn may attend. County and state school officials are desirous of making such a change. President Womer has secured permission of the board of trustees of Washburn College to provide quarters on the campus for the school.

There has been much discussion of such a plan for several years but now is the first time definite plans have been made. The plan is to provide a high class eudcational institution for students of high school age from the College Hill districts between Gage Park and College Hill, and also the districts between the Pauline line and the campus. The students from these districts would pay no tuition, the expense being borne by the various districts. If such a plan as this

still lay outside the Topeka city limits — and be transformed into a high school supported by taxpayer money.

Within months, the deed was done. The trustees approved the shift, patrons of the adjoining areas voted to accept the school as their own, and Washburn High School became a fact. The new entity opened in fall 1918 with 135 students. Ties with Washburn remained strong, however. For the next two decades, the high school would operate from campus space rented to it by the college. Over the same time, the president of its school board would also be the president of Washburn.

The Great War

In the midst of the struggle by Womer and the trustees to smooth out college finances, world events intervened. The war that had engaged most of Europe since 1914 spilled over to the United States, which entered the conflict in April 1917. Across America, life was sure to change, and nowhere more so than on college campuses with their legions of military-age young men.

Class schedules were changed and sessions shortened. Male students were organized into two companies for daily drill of one and a half hours, led by faculty with military experience.

To prepare for service in military hospitals, women had to take courses in first aid and elementary hygiene. Wages of their Red Cross teachers were paid by collections taken up by the YWCA, sororities and dormitory residents.

Attendance at commencement exercises that June fell noticeably below that of years past because many seniors already had enlisted. Some had volunteered for officer training at Fort Riley.

Before the beginning of fall semester 1917, Washburn organized an ambulance company from current students, recent graduates and Kansans from other private colleges in the state. When the time came in mid-September for the company to board the train for Camp Pike near Little Rock, Arkansas, the college staged a picnic for them. Eventually, the company would number more than 120 men and would be trained to shuttle wounded soldiers from field hospitals to base hospitals. From Arkansas, it would be moved to Fort Dix, New Jersey, and it would not arrive in Europe until late in the war. When it did, most of its members were dispersed among other health and medical companies.

The war reduced Washburn's male population noticeably, and not solely because of enlistments in the military. The departure to war of working men from farms, factories and offices opened up jobs on the home front. Employers increased wages to fill them, luring some college men away from classes and into the work force.

German language classes, once among the most popular of Washburn's foreign-language courses, were "basically discredited," according to *The Review*. Since 1914, the beginning of the war in Europe, enrollment in German had dropped by about two-thirds.

With many other American colleges and universities, Washburn applied in mid-1918 for a unit of the Student Army Training Corps. SATC was aimed not only at preparing students for military life but also at providing a military "outlet" in hopes of keeping young men on campus as long as possible and out of recruiting stations. SATC enrollment began

...life was sure to change — and nowhere more so than on college campuses with their legions of military-age young men.

Salutes for Student Army Training Corps inductees on October 1, 1918, in front of Thomas Gymnasium.

that fall. The aim was to provide 10 hours of military training a week, six in drill and marksmanship and four in military-related classes.

To meet military needs, the college switched to a three-term academic year. Authority over students, an important role for college administrators of the day, was divided between Washburn faculty and staff on the one hand and officers assigned by the government on the other.

For Washburn, as well as for other colleges and universities, the experience with SATC proved bumpy. President Womer complained that campus discipline now fell to "very young officers who had little sympathy for or knowledge of college life." SATC also strained the budget. Although the government furnished uniforms and supplies, Washburn had to construct temporary barracks equipped with kitchens, mess rooms and office equipment. The college found that the government reimbursed less than half the cost of that work.

Indeed, SATC got up and running only briefly. In fall 1918, the worldwide flu epidemic reached the Washburn campus. All classes were suspended for two weeks, then re-started and then suspended again. With the second suspension all students, SATC members included, were sent home. The outbreak caused only one fatality at Washburn, a SATC student from Mayetta, Kansas, but throughout Topeka more than 3,900 residents suffered from the illness. About two hundred Topekans died. By January 1919, the *Washburn Bulletin* reported, the epidemic had been "successfully checked."

On November 11, 1918, the armistice in Europe ended the war and also the need for SATC. The unit was disbanded in early December, after less than three months in existence. Administrators and faculty considered the experiment a failure. Drill and exercises

Top: The Washburn Ambulance Company lined up for its group portrait at Camp Pike, Arkansas, in 1917.

Above, trenches, barbed wire and other obstacles filled the Student Army Training Corps field in fall 1918.

got the college men in good shape physically, but not academically. The experience perhaps colored Washburn's attitude toward having an ROTC unit; it would be three decades before one was established on campus.

With the Great War over, things might have returned to normal, but nowhere in America was that the case. The war had changed too much in the minds of too many people. The decade ahead would show just how much.

Facing page: Barracks for the short-lived SATC.

Modern Times to Hard Times

In 1921, the dean of women reported to the president on the ways of Washburn students:

"The college is not what it was a few years ago," wrote Dean Susan Guild. "The war introduced many problems...with more students — many of whom do not come for an education but for a social life."

Faculty, too, stirred the pot. Some professors strenuously and publicly challenged administrators, demanding a larger part in governing the college.

For educators who began their careers when authority went unquestioned, the socially turbulent years after World War I were jarring. Yet for Washburn, they were also years of big plans and big expectations, matching America's new and expansive mood.

In 1918, the United States had ended the greatest war in world history by injecting soldiers, material and money into an exhausted Europe. Now, with the return of veterans, America stood at the threshold of an energetic decade. Across the country in the 1920s, factories hummed and new buildings rose. Automobiles, now affordable by the middle class, poured off assembly lines. Commercial radio stations sprang up, electric power and telephone service extended even into remote areas, and the stock market climbed and climbed. All of that happened amid a pervasive and persuasive wave of product advertising.

College life in general symbolized the free-spending and free-thinking era. Washburn's enrollments climbed, faculty salaries rose and the college's donors loosened their pocketbooks. Like other

Numbers

Population, 1930

- Kansas: 1,880,999
- Topeka: 64,120

Facing page: 1930s skywatchers manipulated the steel-tubed telescope acquired in 1901 as part of the donation for the Crane Observatory, above. Washburn was proud of the device, built by the Warner & Swasey Company of Cleveland. It had won an award at a Paris exposition and was considered among the finest telescopes of the early 20th century.

institutions of higher education, Washburn laid plans for new buildings and new endeavors. To build enthusiasm among students and alumni, Washburn — as did colleges from Harvard to Notre Dame to Southern California — devoted great efforts to fielding winning teams and to building new stadiums and arenas in the exploding worlds of athletics, notably football.

Roaring through the '20s

Washburn reflected a booming America. By 1923, the college listed 600 students in Arts and Sciences, 185 in music, 100 in art and 90 in law, totaling 975. Two hundred forty-six more were enrolled in night school, entering its 10th year of serving students who had full-time day jobs. All classes were now at college level because Washburn no longer served as a preparatory school. Washburn High School, though still renting space on the college campus, had its own tax base and its own administration. Even so, the two institutions had close ties: Womer and his successor as president of the college were elected to head the board that ran the high school.

"Co-educational colleges were not founded for the sake of making them match-making institutions."

— Dean Susan Guild

For American colleges, the decade marked a new era in student behavior. *The Washburn Review* condemned the "lax moral standards which came with the war and have been growing steadily worse," among them "suggestive, daring and immoderate dress and the accompanying evils."

In her report to President Womer, Dean Guild rued "jazz music" and the "style of dancing" that accompanied it, each representing a trend toward looser rules for conduct. Meanwhile, she sought to remind students, female or male, to keep courtship in perspective.

"Co-educational colleges were not founded for the sake of making them match-making institutions," she said.

Women who lived in dormitories were required to return by midnight, or by 12:30 a.m. on nights of parties, and the parties had to be authorized by Washburn.

As one of the prime symbols of the decade's frantic pace, fraternities and sororities grew. Some of their members' free-spending habits contributed to a notion spreading in Kansas that Washburn had become a "rich man's school." Doing nothing to dispel that idea, *The Review* complained in 1920 that random parking of automobiles on campus had become a problem. Before the 1920s, few students could have afforded a car.

Chapel remained compulsory, as befitted a college still church-related, but even there students grew rambunctious. Some chapel speakers had difficulty talking above shuffling feet and a rumble of conversations.

Students often violated campus bans on smoking. At one point in the 1920s, the faculty declared the Ichabod Inn off-limits for smoking. The Inn was the old Hartford Cottage converted into a common area with food service, a post office and meeting rooms. It was a popular gathering spot and the smoking prohibition met stiff resistance from students. The Student Council declared that students ought to have the right to smoke anywhere. Eventually, a compromise allowed the practice only during certain hours.

That led to this poem, as published in *The Review*:

Have you ever been at the College Inn
at a quarter after ten?
Then you've doubtless seen through a smoky
screen that bunch of college men.
Now each one there tries to do his share
To pollute the atmosphere...

By the end of the decade, the college agreed to demands to allow smoking anywhere, at any time.

In 1922, the Student Council, which had been established in 1912, discussed the question of "better dancing and better dance music" and recommended that Greek organizations carefully supervise their dances. The council had clout in the matter; in those days it acted as the clearinghouse for the timing of

Professor vs. president

By the late 1910s, the foundations of authority in America were quaking. In industry, workers sought changes in working conditions and sometimes went on strike. In higher education, restive faculty agitated for a greater say in how colleges were run. Washburn figured prominently in that struggle.

On one side stood some members of the Washburn faculty whose spokesman was a history and political science professor, John Ervin Kirkpatrick. On the other side stood the administration and Board of Trustees, represented by President Parley Womer.

At issue was decision-making power. For his part, Kirkpatrick complained that President Womer acted dictatorially and showed interest not in the college as a teaching institution but mainly in his promises to the trustees to raise money. Fundraising ventures often took Womer away from campus, the professor said, adding that he continually submitted ideas for change to Womer but that the president had proven "too old and too busy to learn." At the time Womer was nearing 50. Eventually, Kirkpatrick would call Womer morally bankrupt.

The professor, J.E. Kirkpatrick, top, squared off with the president, Parley Womer.

Womer, for his part, described Professor Kirkpatrick as insubordinate, revolutionary, tactless, officious — and generally a nuisance.

Kirkpatrick, who held a master's degree from Yale and had been a Congregational minister in Kansas, joined the Washburn faculty in spring 1908 as field secretary. In April 1909, he became an assistant professor of history and also taught political science. After a few years Kirkpatrick began to carve out an assertive reputation for himself with administrators and particularly with Womer once the latter became president in 1915. From time to time, the professor went around Womer directly to certain trustees, to the press and to public officials.

At one point, Kirkpatrick proposed to Womer a curriculum in business administration, which Womer acknowledged would be a good idea — sometime in the future. To Womer's chagrin, Kirkpatrick promptly took the proposal, complete with course outline and roster of instructors, to Topeka business leaders. Several of them pronounced it a fine suggestion. Womer then had to explain to them why the plan would not work, at least not right away.

Perhaps most annoying to the president were Kirkpatrick's efforts to organize the faculty under the American Federation of Teachers, which Womer was certain would annoy anti-union contributors in the business community.

Matters came to a head in June 1919, when the Board of Trustees, at Womer's urging, asked Kirkpatrick to resign. Afterward, Womer offered Kirkpatrick a hearing before the board, but Kirkpatrick rejected the move as inadequate. The professor rebuked Womer, writing him, "Your last day's service for Washburn will be your best day."

Kirkpatrick was dismissed.

The American Association of University Professors took up Kirkpatrick's cause, sending a representative to investigate. His report appeared in 1921, condemning Womer and, by extension, the Washburn Board of Trustees.

Kirkpatrick taught for a year at Harvard and later the University of Michigan and Olivet College, a small institution in Michigan. From there, he wrote to foundations that contributed to Washburn, urging them to encourage the college to reorganize itself to give a greater voice to alumni and faculty.

With time passions cooled. In December 1929, still espousing his beliefs but now in failing health, Kirkpatrick wrote Womer. He acknowledged making "more than one mistake" in the disputatious period at Washburn.

"But there is one in particular which I have come to regret more than the others: That I did not accept your hearty and evidently well-meant invitation for a hearing before the board.

"Also, and still more important, I regret the unkind feelings I have, until of late, allowed myself to entertain toward you."

In early 1931, Kirkpatrick died at a house on College Avenue in Topeka. His estate left $10,000 to Washburn College for a faculty trust fund, to be administered by faculty.

1919: The Law School began a four-year course, the first year of which included largely standard college courses and ended in a law degree.
– 124 law students moved to a remodeled Holbrook Hall, which since 1886 had been used as a women's dormitory.
1923: Benton Hall was constructed for a women's dormitory.
1924: Mulvane Art Museum opened.
1925: The Law School required two years of college work for admission.
1927: Washburn changed its grading nomenclature. Out went S for Superior, G for Good, M for Medium, I for Inferior and C for Conditional. In came A, B, C, D. and E, the last representing incomplete work or a conditional grade. In 1935, F for Failure would be added to the list.
– Trustees set a retirement age of 70 for employees.
1928: Whiting Field House and Moore Bowl were built and opened.

Fraternities and sororities

Fraternities and sororities, at their best, eased the path through college for members by providing social interaction, a feeling of belonging and mutual support through personal and academic problems. By sponsoring social events, they also eased interaction between the sexes. Even after graduation, the groups helped their members form business associations and other networks that might last a lifetime.

But the groups also came under criticism from administrators, faculty, independent students and people outside the college. Much criticism centered on the way they treated members in waiting, or pledges. "Hell week" was considered a serious disruption of a freshman's academic pursuits. Reports and rumors about hazing practices such as paddling and harsh criticism drew complaints that that the practices were infantile at best and sadistic at worst.

"Rush," when potential new members were selected, could be a particularly troublesome time among sororities. Accusers said some of the recruitment was accomplished through "talking down" other sororities, and sometimes the allegations got so bad that students withdrew from college.

These fraternity pledges underwent traditional paddling in 1929.

Well-founded or not, the administration feared that the allegations might damage Washburn's chances among voters in the 1941 municipalization election. As part of the campaign to pass the tax levy and "municipalize" Washburn, administrators counseled fraternities and sororities to convince the public that the groups made a "genuine contribution." The social groups also were encouraged to end hazing, show respect to pledges and alter "wholesale and mechanical" group-study requirements — which served mainly to help members pass tests.

1930: Washburn installed lights in Moore Bowl for night games, the second college in Kansas to do so after Haskell in Lawrence. "There is no difficulty," the *Washburn College Bulletin* said, "in seeing the highest punts and passes."
1931: Parley Womer resigned as president and chaired the American Citizenship program. He was replaced by Phillip King.
– A nine-hole golf course for students and the public was built on south and west sides of campus.
1933: Former Washburn President Frank Sanders died.
1939: In June, the first Sunflower Girls State took place at Washburn with 150 high school-age girls recommended by their principals or teachers. Girls State was instituted three years after Boys State, which then took place at the University of Wichita. Both were weeklong programs created by the American Legion to give youth an opportunity to learn about government and also to respect and preserve it. Girls State moved to the University of Kansas in Lawrence in 1941.
1940: Faced with terrific financial difficulty, the Board of Trustees voted to close Washburn unless something was done to save it.
– The Law School moved to Boswell Hall.

dances, Greek or non-Greek.

Faculty did not go unquestioned, either. In 1924, the Student Council moved to petition instructors to recognize students' right to leave class when the period expired — regardless of whether instructors wanted to continue. After all, another instructor would be waiting for his or her own class to begin.

Students also enacted their own rules, many to the detriment of underclassmen. Freshmen men were supposed to wear blue caps and freshman women armbands. Upperclassmen were expected to enforce the rule, at least until the Thanksgiving break each year.

In 1924, some young, able-bodied people began carrying canes. They were senior law students, who that year decided that the practice would distinguish them on sight. Engineering students took to wearing high boots, Army-style britches and wool shirts in celebration of the outdoorsy nature of their chosen profession.

For a while, literary societies remained alive and well, meeting on Fridays. Public speaking was the first order — the men's Gamma Sigma Literary Society provided debaters and orators — but literature, art and music were part of the package, too. Women's societies were Alethean, Helianthus and Washburn Girls'. All stocked the women's and men's debate teams.

Bleachers were nearly full at the campus field and cheerleaders stood ready for action at a game in 1923.

As they had since the late 19th century, some Washburn students savored the chance to stand in front of a group and speak, or argue, or harangue. As evidence, there was the 1925 debate squad — seven men and seven women — which scheduled 25 intercollegiate matches with institutions ranging from the University of Southern California on the west to the University of West Virginia on the east and several in between.

Although Washburn dropped public

Keeping "warriors on the field"

The student-athletes of the 1920s had trouble keeping up with classwork, as did later generations. Among organizations and clubs featured in the 1925 *Kaw* is the Ichabod First Aiders. The first aid they provided was for "moments of scholastic danger," when they were to tutor the athletes "and thus keep the warriors on the field." The group, advised by Librarian Jesse Dean, had two men and six women.

The football players, however, didn't keep up their end of the bargain, losing seven of the eight games they played in 1925. The 1924-1925 basketball team, on the other hand, went undefeated and won the National AAU tournament in Kansas City. Their coach was A.C. "Dutch" Lonborg, under whom Washburn would repeat as conference champions in the 1925-1926 season.

In the years between the wars, Washburn football prospered in the two coaching stints of Ernest Bearg. He was coach in 1918 and 1919, and compiled an 11-2-1 record, and again from 1929 to 1935. Washburn went 35-31-3 in that time and won the Central Conference championship in 1930.

In 1935, Washburn began a brief run in the Missouri Valley Conference. The football team had winning records only in 1938 and 1940, after which Washburn withdrew from the conference in an attempt to save money. In basketball, Washburn had only two winning seasons in the Missouri Valley and no championships.

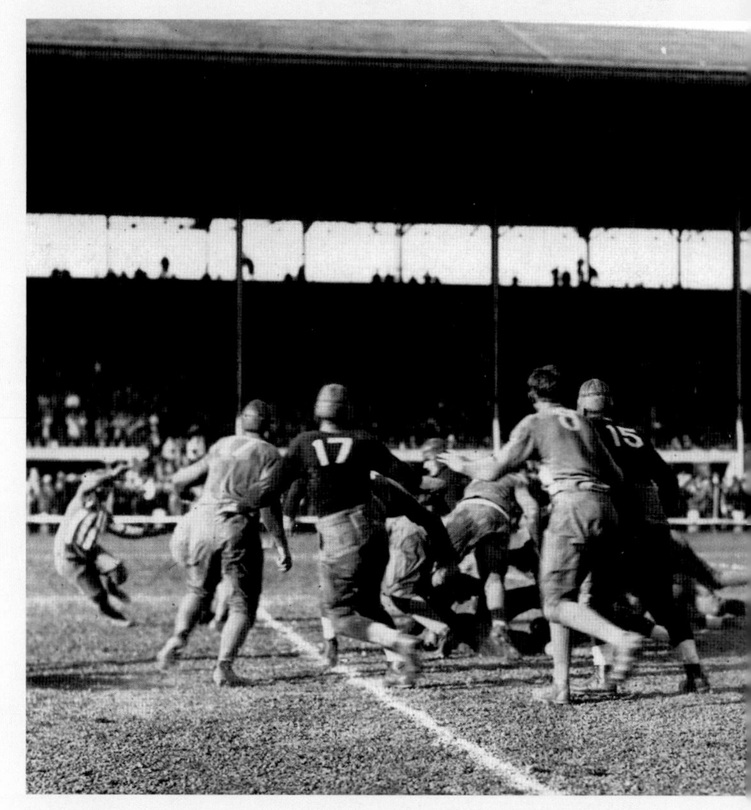

Top: The Washburn basketball team went undefeated and won the Amateur Athletic Union tournament in 1925. Above, the football team played its home games at the Shawnee County fairgrounds from 1924 to 1927.

Left: A Washburn runner won the 220-yard dash at the conference track meet in 1933.

In 1930, freshmen played sophomores in a class-vs.-class game on Hobo Day at the old athletic field next to 17th Street.

speaking as a required course, students still signed up and filled four fundamental sections. New to the campus in 1925 was extemporaneous speaking, and Washburn won a four-way contest in that oratorical art against Kansas State, Emporia, Bethany and Ottawa.

All manner of other clubs existed, among them French, biology, engineering, and even a club for out-of-town women who were neither sorority members nor lived on campus.

Others liked to sing, for which there were men's and women's glee clubs. The band, all male in 1925, was uniformed in white pants and high-collar coats with military-style hats and performed for football games. The Washburn orchestra, meanwhile, gave three concerts in MacVicar Chapel.

Fight, team!

The 1920s has been labeled a Golden Age of sports in the United States. Babe Ruth in baseball, Jack Dempsey in boxing and Man o' War in horse-racing caught the imaginations of Americans. Newspaper sportswriters happily fueled the fires, and so did broadcasters on the new medium, radio.

At colleges, football was king but basketball was growing in popularity.

Fans got themselves organized, or tried to. In 1920, *The Washburn Review* rued that exuberant students seemed unable to chant together on "Hold that line!" The newspaper published a letter signed by "a cheer leader" who tried to help: "The first words of the 'Washburn Who' should come when the fists of the cheer leaders are at their ears.... 'Yea Washburn' will be started when the clenched left hands of the leaders are extended to the left."

Cheers were supposed to remain positive, and rattling the opponents would not be tolerated. Twice in one football game, referees had to admonish Washburn students for yelling so loudly that the Ottawa University players couldn't hear their own signals.

"True sportsmanship," *The Review* said, "does not consist of repeated attempts to confuse the plans of the opponent."

Victories sometimes drove students into a frenzy. After Washburn beat St. Mary's in 1920 and won the conference football championship, a game that took place on a Thursday, students roamed Kansas Avenue in groups,

Whiting Field House seated several thousand for basketball games and other indoor events, top and right. Above: The man who made it possible, A.B. Whiting, who had been a Washburn trustee.

noisily poking into picture shows and dance halls. The next morning, groups of young people "whip cracked" through classrooms. A week later, in a meeting at the chapel, the students were admonished in a friendly way by President Womer. The students resolved that their "lawlessness was regretted."

But rowdiness never went out of fashion. In 1928, in the week leading up to the first football game at the new Moore Bowl, a group of students organized a "shirt tail" parade to downtown Topeka. Things got out of hand. At Topeka High School, celebrators disrupted some classes. Also, they damaged a labor union sign and, back on campus, invaded Benton Hall. Administrators and faculty demanded an apology and payment for damages. The Student Council acceded, issuing the apology and levying a 10-cent assessment on students.

Places to play

The high-flying 1920s encouraged institutions to place big bets on the future. Across the country, colleges and universities built new football stadiums and indoor arenas. Washburn held out until later in the decade, and then made its decision to construct a new $200,000-plus complex as a home for athletics. A fundraising campaign would pay for it all.

The football team — which had played on a field in the northwest quadrant of the campus in front of bleachers so decrepit that spectators occasionally fell through the footboards, and later at the fairgrounds — would have a new stadium.

Basketball, which gave Washburn something to cheer about through Kansas winters, would get a field house that also would serve other indoor sports — swimming, boxing, wrestling, handball and volleyball. Included also was a stage for theatrical productions and concerts.

The new football stadium took shape in the mind of a Washburn engineering professor, Cleveland Loper. He devised a plan to excavate a draw or depression that was a natural feature in a meadow south of the main campus buildings. His own classes got the assignment for the earliest work: surveying the area. Their next task was to draw up a plan, and in 1923 the students devised how the stadium would be built — at a fraction of the cost of one constructed on level ground.

The idea never went beyond the conceptual stage in Loper's classes until the fundraising campaign gained momentum. The plan for a new bowl attached itself to the plan for the more costly field house and by spring 1928 excavation was well under way. Dirt from the

Moore Bowl in 1930, part of a proud new array of athletic facilities.

middle of what would become the football field was excavated and graded into gentle slopes on either side.

Once the "bowl" was created, seating was constructed on the slopes, thus saving money on structural support. Students provided some of the construction labor. Expectations were for it to seat 7,000 to 8,000 with the capability of increasing capacity to 15,000.

The fundraising pledge drive succeeded and on September 29, 1928, Washburn played its first game on the new field against William Jewell College of Liberty, Missouri. In the weeks before the game, the trustees named the field for George Godfrey Moore of Topeka, a Topeka insurance executive and Washburn booster. Despite the rowdy nightshirt parade the week before and ceremonies on opening day, the home team lost, 20-12.

On December 18, 1928, the new limestone field house was dedicated. In the pregame ceremony, KU basketball coach Forrest "Phog" Allen called it "the finest college field house in the Middle West." In Lawrence, Allen's own team played in a multipurpose auditorium.

According to Washburn, the new field house could hold 3,000 to 5,000 spectators — although the biggest crowds were typically cited at 2,500. In the first game, Washburn played its rivals down the Kaw, Allen's Kansas Jayhawks, and beat KU, 25-24. In 1930 the structure was renamed Whiting Field House

Engineering students, dressed in rugged outdoor gear, surveyed the site of the football stadium as a class project.

Washburn's new Mulvane Art Museum in the middle 1920s.

The Mulvane: A "proper" place for works of art

Impressed by the work of a Washburn art instructor, wealthy Topekan Joab R. Mulvane pledged $50,000 in 1922 to build a new museum and expanded facilities for the Art Department.

The donation resulted from the efforts of the department director, Frances Dean Whittemore. She inspired the creation of the Topeka Art Guild, brought art exhibitions to town and cultivated the interest of wealthy art enthusiasts. Mulvane had spent his career in Kansas building railroads, dealing in land, oil, salt, natural gas, banking and other pursuits and then turned to philanthropy.

In early 1922, the contract was awarded to build a three-floor, Italian Renaissance-style structure. It opened to the public January 13, 1924, having cost $60,000. Various accounts have called it the first museum in Kansas designed for the "proper" showing of paintings. Others have said it was the oldest accredited art museum west of the Mississippi.

In 1931, the museum staged an exhibit of the works of John Steuart Curry. It was the first major exposure of the Kansas-born artist's work to his fellow Kansans, and drew complaints that he depicted his native state too harshly. Some of Curry's art on exhibit contained a tornado, a flood and a lynch mob. Those reactions presaged complaints about the murals he would create at the Capitol in 1941.

In the tornado of 1966, the Mulvane survived but its roof and windows were damaged. Within a few years the structure was gutted and connected to a new Garvey Fine Arts Center, which houses music and theater departments.

after longtime college trustee and benefactor Albe Burge Whiting.

An art center and other upgrades

Like many cities west of the Mississippi, Topeka in the 1920s had no art gallery, public or private, a fact bemoaned in the newspapers and by the local Art Guild. To remedy the situation, Topekan Joab Mulvane stepped forward with a donation to build a museum on the Washburn campus.

Ever on the lookout for more contributions from Washburn's wealthiest supporters President Womer proposed to Otis L. Benton, a northwest Kansas banker, Washburn alumnus of the class of 1884 and member of the Board of Trustees, that he help build a new women's dormitory. In return, the wealthy Benton would see his family name on the building. As happened often through the 1920s, Womer proved persuasive and the college got a $50,000 gift from Benton. In 1923, Benton Hall opened. It could house 100 women students.

Meanwhile, the main drive through campus was paved, buildings reconditioned and new equipment bought.

At the time, the building program of the 1920s was called the largest ever undertaken by the college at one time.

The college ended the decade with new departments of Home Economics, Business Administration and American Citizenship. In fall semester 1929 Washburn raised its tuition 20 percent, from $75 a semester to $90.

The 1920s proved good for Washburn, as they did throughout the United States. Rightly proud of the new facilities and the favorable attention they brought to the school, Washburn's faculty, staff, students and alumni expected a solid future into the 1930s.

However, events that were about to unfold would turn those expectations on their head.

The crash and a departure

Even as so much of American business prospered through the 1920s, there was one major exception: the farm economy. Overproduction, a result of 20th-century technological advances in farm machinery and agricultural techniques, dampened prices for crops and cattle. Washburn's endowment, much of it invested in farmland and mortgages, suffered nagging reminders through the otherwise heady 1920s. A national farm loan law further limited college revenues by helping lower the rate of interest on loans, and thus on some proceeds of the endowment.

Indeed, through most of the 1910s and 1920s, operating revenue from tuition and endowment income fell substantially short of expenses. Trustees and administrators, as they had throughout the history of Washburn, found ways to keep the college going. To overcome annual operating deficits, the college borrowed from outsiders and put its own holdings on the market. In 1925, the college sold tracts it owned across Kansas to pay off $125,000 in loans to three Topeka banks. By doing so, Washburn lost any further possibilities of generating income from them.

Washburn had become like a family whose breadwinners' paychecks and investment income consistently fell short of its spending. Each year, such a family would have to borrow or beg money, or withdraw cash from its investments.

October 1929 brought bad news across the country. U.S. stock markets tumbled, a signal

Living room of Benton Hall, a women's dormitory, in the 1930s.

1916

"HOBO" DAY IS
INSTITUTED HER

A CHAPTER OF THE ANCIEN
ORDER OF SONS OF REST
INSTALLED.

Annual Meeting to Be Held Ju
Before Every K. U.-Washburn
Game.

Washburn had a "tacky" day las
Friday. No Coxey's Army, band c
I. W. W.'s or itinerant tramps eve
paralleled the horde of Weary Wi
lies that swarmed over the campu
and took the administration of a
fairs in their own hands last Frida
morning. Classes were dismissed a
11:30 o'clock and the mob ruled su
preme.

Yes, Algernon, it was all plotte
nd planned the day before. On th
ay preceding the Kansas game
as deemed advisable to devise som
vel means of arousing mor
p" than has ever been shown be
. Consequently Angelus Burch
unequaled President of th
ers' Club, started his imagina
faculties to functioning and th
was the plan of having eac
very male in the college ap
t school on Friday garbed i
ckiest" rags possible, a veile
of the consequences of no
this plan, was given also.

A celebration in rags

Hobo Day began in 1916 to generate pep for the upcoming football game against the University of Kansas. Organizers encouraged male students to dress the "hickest" they could. By 1927 crowds of poorly clad collegians — by then including women — posed with Governor Ben Paulsen, above. Hobo Day, later combined with homecoming, continued in various forms into the 1980s. Left: Hobo king and queen in the 1930s.

that the business boom of the 1920s was going bust. Afterward came business failures and bank closures, and America fell into a general economic slowdown. Incomes and fortunes shrank and even evaporated, and many of Washburn's donors found that pledges they had made to build the new athletics complex in the fast-growing days of 1927 and 1928 had become unsustainable burdens.

For Parley Womer, the battle was becoming difficult. In the decade and a half since he became president of the college, Womer had ridden a wave of success in fundraising that helped maintain the balance sheet. But as the country entered the Great Depression and donors' generosity diminished, Womer found that squeezing more promises out of alumni and friends of the college, not to mention the task of running it, took a personal toll.

Womer had let the trustees know in 1925 that he wanted his contract to last only five more years, until 1930, at which point he would have served 16 years as president. In June 1929, Womer confirmed that intention by submitting his resignation to the Board of Trustees, effective August 31, 1930. He cited the "pressures of fundraising and the growing burden of administration." However, the trustees would not accept it.

Then Womer's health forced the issue. In early 1930, he suffered what the *Washburn Bulletin* described as a physical breakdown attributed to the press of his duties. Womer himself described it as "a result of my over-strenuous year at Washburn." He spent that summer in California, resting. Womer sought to return to work for the fall semester but his doctors overruled him, recommending instead a leave of absence of several months.

Needing someone to run the place during Womer's recovery, the trustees created a new position, associate president, and hired Phillip C. King for the job. He began work in

A chance meeting and the matter of American Citizenship

On a snowy night in 1916, Parley Womer was traveling through New England, seeking the kind of people who might donate substantial sums to his faraway Washburn College. This night, he happened to be in Worcester, Massachusetts, where Ichabod Washburn lived when he made his important donation in 1868.

In a blinding snowstorm, as Womer later told the story, he lost his way and so knocked on the front door of a house to ask directions. Invited in, he found that the owner was one George Alden, descendant of John Alden of Mayflower fame. The latter-day Alden, a Harvard graduate, had taught mechanical engineering and been a consultant. He also was involved in banking and eventually headed an abrasives-manufacturing company employing 5,000 people. All this brought him sizable wealth.

Womer soon discovered that George Alden was interested in the future of his country and its youth. He told Alden that he meant to establish at Washburn a Department of American Citizenship, which, he pointed out, would serve Alden's dreams precisely. He knew of no other college department like it. Alden was intrigued.

The result of the chance meeting and subsequent communications between Alden and Womer and the Washburn trustees was a pledge by Alden of $100,000 to a program that would carry his name. The gift was equal to more than $1 million in 21st-century dollars.

The plan was announced to the public in 1925. It included a deal with Womer, under which he would continue as college president for five years and then become head of the new department, which would teach history and political science and other courses. By 1928, the American Citizenship Department was instituted and Womer reported to the trustees of Alden's estate — the benefactor died in 1926 — that more than 200 young people had enrolled. The Alden trustees pronounced themselves satisfied, and in 1929 they finished turning over the $100,000.

In 1931 Womer, having stepped down as Washburn president, took over the program and began campaigning for the ideal it represented, which he described as improving the quality of thinking and action on the part of American citizens — rather than altering forms of government. Also, the program aimed to help integrate immigrants into the American mainstream.

However, by 1938 the American Citizenship program was foundering. A study by the Washburn trustees criticized several instructors as poor teachers. It described Womer himself as "sadly disillusioned" and isolated from colleagues and from the Washburn administration. Womer held on for a while, defending his stewardship of the program by virtue of his being the person who raised the money from George Alden.

But soon Womer, disagreeing with proposed changes in the American Citizenship program, offered to resign and the trustees accepted. Afterward Womer continued to defend the program, and in the wake of municipalization in 1941 aroused managers of the Alden estate by claiming the new university shortchanged the American Citizenship effort.

Nevertheless, the program would continue for decades as the umbrella for the Washburn history and political science departments.

...Womer...described [the program] as improving the quality of thinking and action on the part of American citizens — rather than altering forms of government.

American Citizenship tour bus, 1932: Taking the message throughout Kansas.

The Washburn marching band, 1938.

April 1930.

On June 1, 1931, Womer officially notified the trustees that he found it impossible to continue as president and would step down effective September 1.

The trustees promptly chose King to replace him as of the fall semester in 1931.

Though no longer president, Womer had recovered sufficiently to continue working at Washburn. He was named head of the new department of American Citizenship, which would oversee courses in history and political science. Also, he was named to the Washburn Board of Trustees. Womer and his wife arranged to build a new house — a distinctive, California Mission-style structure with tile roof — on the campus. The trustees allowed the couple to occupy it for their lifetimes, after which it would become college property.

President Womer's on-campus residence.

Decade of difficulty

Phillip King, the man who replaced Womer, was an Ohioan, educated at Oberlin College in Ohio, where his father had been president, and Columbia University in New York. In the World War, King had served as a chaplain. He had been pastor of Congregational churches in Cleveland, Toledo and Dayton, Ohio and had helped run an endowment campaign for Ohio Wesleyan.

Now in his early 40s, King took over an office and a college shadowed by the Great Depression, which was settling in for a long stay. Its effects would follow King until he left office.

Despite King's being another in a line of Congregationalist ministers who served as president of Washburn, the denomination in which King and his predecessors had spent much of their lives continued to offer little support for its collegiate creation. In the early 1920s, Parley Womer reported that, in a campaign to raise half a million dollars, Congregational churches had supplied about $25,000, or 5 percent. Nor had the churches stepped forward in the remainder of the decade. One study found that most denominations gave their related colleges about 3 to 4 percent of their benevolent contributions — but Congregationalists gave only about 1 percent.

Home economics lab in Rice Hall, 1930.

Womer's successor acknowledged that ties with the church were weak.

"Washburn has been functioning for a good many years," he wrote in 1934, "as an independent liberal arts college with a Christian tradition, rather than as a denominational college."

Only one in 10 Washburn students listed themselves as Congregationalists.

"We have a good many more Methodists and Presbyterians," King wrote," than those from Congregationalist homes."

Chapel attendance remained compulsory into the 1930s, although by 1938 the college was considering making the services voluntary.

Phillip King

In 1931 Edwin B. Dean of Doane College — a Nebraska institution that also was founded by Congregationalists — had given a speech about church colleges vs. public institutions.

"The curse of the tax-supported institution," Dean said, "is politics. The curse of the church college is poverty."

Washburn administrators understood the sentiment. Running ever more in the red, they pleaded for contributions and dug into donations that had been made without restrictions on the principal. But the Great Depression struck blow after blow.

The proud campus building program of the Roaring '20s had been financed by borrowing, which included an issue of $200,000 in bonds in 1927. Depression or no Depression, the college owed regular interest payments of 5 percent to the bondholders, and also owed regular payments to banks for additional loans. The entire bond issue, including principal, was to be paid off after 15 years, which meant the college would have a big payment to make in 1942.

Meanwhile, money from pledges gathered

Washburn's objectives

In March 1936, President Phillip King took the lectern at weekly chapel service to summarize the purposes of the college. The goals he listed were drawn up by Arthur Sellen, the dean of liberal arts, modified by a committee and reviewed by the entire faculty. Washburn's purposes, it was decided, were these:

Establish and maintain physical and mental health.

Secure at least a fair degree of competence in the use of the English, and acquaintance with at least one foreign language.

Make clear the scientific method.

Aid students to understand, appreciate and make use of the heritage of the past.

Enable students to get some understanding of philosophy, psychology and religion, and their bearing upon the problems of reality and living.

Give each student special competence in a specific field....

Prepare students for professional and graduate activity.

Furnish students...vocational guidance.

Meet the educational needs of mature and employed persons.

Help each student establish satisfying relations with his fellows.

Instill in the minds of students a sense of social responsibility and give motivation for conduct which advances the public weal.

in the campaign to build the new structures never equaled the college's annual operating deficits. Hoped-for revenue from athletics — crowds flocking to Moore Bowl and the field house for games — did not flow in as expected. The burden created by the bond issue to build the field house and football stadium pushed the deficit, in King's words, "to alarming proportions."

A big slice of the college's endowment — $350,000 — was invested in farm mortgages. By the end of the 1930s farm loans returned barely 1 percent a year, and yielded $10,000 to $20,000 a year less than the college received in 1929 and before.

Gifts to pay for current spending shrank with the economy and bequests to the college endowment fell. Fundraising campaigns in 1933 and 1935 did little to stem the bad economic tide. A continuing-gift push, which persuaded about 250 backers of the college to contribute a certain amount each year, also failed to alleviate problems.

In all this, there was one spark of good news. In 1935, a decades-long wait for the estate of Charles Boswell to open up finally ended with a court settlement freeing a bequest that amounted to half a million dollars.

"The curse of the tax-supported institution is politics. The curse of the church college is poverty."

— Edwin B. Dean

Boswell, a 19th-century Connecticut grocer, banker and insurance executive, had died in 1887 at age 85. He had become interested in struggling colleges and Washburn was one of them. Before his death, he had given $10,000 to help construct the building that would become Boswell Library. He gave $10,000 more in memory of his son, who died as a student at Yale. And he gave the bell that was mounted in Rice Hall's belfry and became a Washburn tradition

His biggest gift, however, would wait half a century because it was tied to the death of his survivors. Part of his estate was to be transferred to the college at the death of his sister and a far larger amount at the death of his daughter. The daughter, however, would live until 1941. So in 1935, Washburn found a way to bring about a settlement that delivered more than $500,000 — worth roughly $8 million in 21st-century dollars — to Washburn's endowment. But even that amount would generate only $18,000 to $20,000 a year in income, not enough to overcome Washburn's operating deficit.

Fundraising campaigns continued into the year of Washburn's 75th anniversary, 1940. They curbed but could not stop the flow of red ink.

Symbolic of the college's trials, in May of the 75th anniversary year Bertha Kirkpatrick, widow of the professor who had championed the cause of faculty rights and distressed Parley Womer, wrote a letter to King. Her late husband had left money for Washburn faculty in his will in 1930, but his estate had "so completely collapsed" that "nothing more tangible than good wishes" was available for Washburn.

The tuition dilemma

Tuitions propped up Washburn's budget, some years amounting to 60 percent of annual revenue. Hard times made it difficult to raise them. Already, Washburn's tuition — increased for the 1929-1930 academic year — was the highest tuition of any college in Kansas.

To be sure, total college expenses were moderated for the majority of Washburn students, who lived with their families in or near Topeka and spent little or nothing on room and board. In 1935, a survey of male

Under pressure

In 1919, Parley Womer had to fend off complaints from an accrediting group that entrance to the Law School was too easy. Washburn strengthened the requirement to four years of high school and one year of college work, yet the accreditors were not satisfied. In 1922, they also declared the law library too small and its contents too limited. In addition, the law dean was spending entirely too much time at a downtown law firm, where he was in private practice.

Again, Washburn Law tightened things up. Beginning in fall 1925, it started a two-year pre-legal plan and in 1931 increased the requirement to three years. By 1929, the law library contained more than 10,000 volumes.

And still it was not enough. In 1930 the accrediting group, the Association of American Law Schools, said the library remained too limited, and added a new complaint: faculty salaries were "entirely inadequate." Indeed, the agency listed problems with the Washburn Law School dating back to 1907 and said the institution had "never satisfactorily lived up to its obligation" as a member.

The Law School faculty, including secretary Emily Platt, in 1921.

Frustrated at the association and suspecting that his own law dean was using the group to "force the hand" of Washburn to grant his requests, Womer considered withdrawing from the group entirely. Before the academic year was out, however, Phillip King replaced Womer as president. King adopted a less adversarial approach to the association and the controversies diminished.

students found that more than two-thirds lived with relatives, most of them parents.

Yet the high tuition took a toll. In the first two years after the tuition increase of 1929-30, as the economy worsened, enrollment declined sharply. Worried administrators poured money into student aid beginning in 1933, and for the next four years the trend reversed itself. By the middle of the decade Washburn was contributing about $29,000 to student aid and enrollments neared 1,000, the highest ever. But with few students paying the full cost, the expenses associated with handling more students offset much of the gain.

As a result, in the late 1930s, scholarships were cut nearly in half. Predictably, enrollment slipped back downward. By 1940, only 739 students were enrolled.

A report on women's housing found that rooms were sitting empty; by 1940 Washburn had only 53 women from out of town, less than half the number of the late 1920s. Benton Hall — built to house 90 women students in the early 1920s, when enrollment of out-of-town women was growing — had only 13 residents.

That same year, admissions officials reported that a new promotion by the University of Kansas calculated Topeka students could commute to Lawrence and pay KU's cheaper tuition for a lower total than staying at home and attending Washburn. Lawrence, after all, was only 30 miles east.

And KU was not the only competitor; Kansas State was about 60 miles west. Also, since 1919, junior colleges had sprung up across Kansas. Over two decades they increasingly siphoned off freshmen and sophomores who might have attended Washburn. Finally, the one-time teachers colleges in Emporia and Pittsburg added new majors that competed with Washburn's.

A bit quieter

With the Depression came a quieter campus. A 1930s graduate of Washburn

Following pages: Thomas Gymnasium with flagpole in the 1930s, Crane Observatory in the background.

Well-forested by the 1930s, the northern part of campus looked this way from the air. The view was to the south.

recalled decades later how things felt:

"Classes were small. A close relationship was developed with professors. Everyone knew everyone else on campus. Many of the students were from Topeka and we had been together since grade school."

There was a bit of evidence that tight times had affected student exuberance — or was it simply changing fashion?

Susan Guild, the same dean of women who condemned the onset of jazz and other edgy conduct in 1921, reported to King in 1935 that student life had improved.

"The jazz music and noise of the earlier years," she said, "has gradually disappeared. Orchestras have given us music of a higher type. Students have done away with their boisterous applause.

"The Depression has produced a better social life and a much less expensive one."

Parties were chaperoned, and it was required that the chaperoning group include at least one faculty member.

"Only at a few parties," she said, had drinking gotten out of hand and "chaperons have been embarrassed and obliged to take a hand."

Dean Guild also believed that Washburn students drank less alcohol than students at other colleges. Smoking, on the other hand, was rampant — "now so universal that it is permitted at parties."

Also nearly universal in social life was the "coming of automobiles in great numbers."

"No young man of today," she wrote, "dares to ask his lady to walk even a block to a party."

As for those sanctioned parties, students were staying only an hour or so for the dancing before leaving for parts unknown.

"They all climb into cars," the dean remarked. "No one knows where they go or

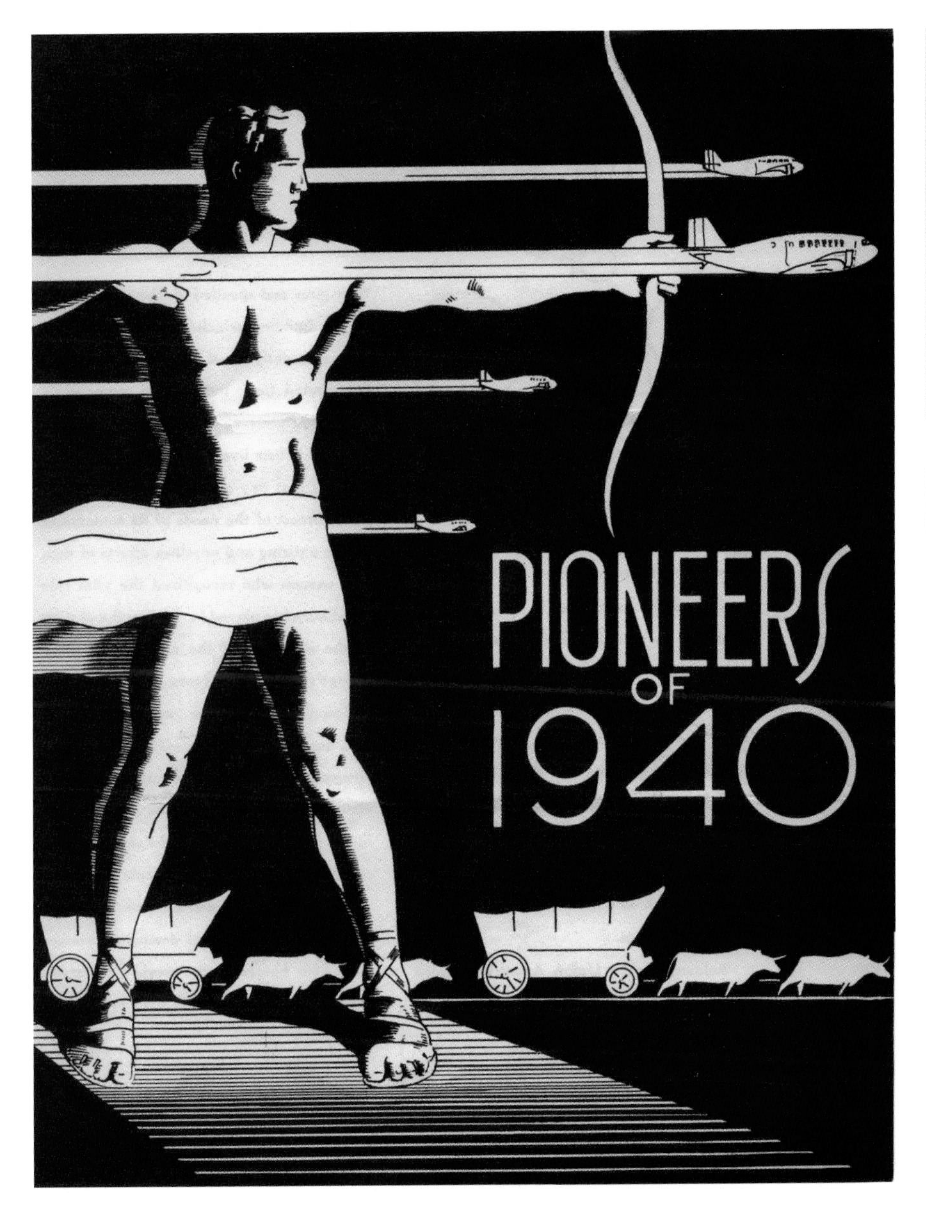

75th Anniversary

Financial difficulties breathed down the neck of the college in 1940, yet Washburn still found the spirit to celebrate 75 years since its founding. Organizers of the celebration created a calendar illustrated with scenes of campus and college symbols. Left: cover of a fundraising brochure.

what they do."

By 1938, word was getting around Topeka that some were going to local night clubs. In a cautionary note, President King wrote to fraternity presidents, "These later sessions seem to have become conspicuous and appear to be causing remark in Topeka."

People were identifying the groups as Washburn students, King continued, in particular those belonging to any fraternity that had scheduled a party that night.

But not everything revolved around fraternities and sororities. In her report to King, the dean of women noted how the literary societies so popular in the 19th century had mostly disappeared, but had been replaced by a multitude of other organizations.

Among them were associations catering to non-fraternity and non-sorority students, thus strengthening the role of independents in campus life. Those groups, like fraternities and sororities, held parties — "and very inexpensive ones."

As a result, independents had reached

Rules for Students, 1937-1938

From "Washburn Faculty Rules":

Students may room only in approved rooming places and will change rooming places during the year only after securing permission from the Dean of Women.

Young women in sorority and rooming houses are expected to observe quiet hours from 8:00 to 12:00 a.m.; from 1:40 to 4:00 p.m. and from 8:00 to 10:30 p.m., and from 10:30 p.m. to 6:30 a.m. Lights are to be out by 11:00 except by special permit of the house mother. Exception is made of Friday, Saturday and Sunday evenings. Gentlemen callers are not to be received and there are to be no engagements during the above quiet hours except by special consent of the house mother.

Young women desiring evening privileges of study in the library are to return home by 10:00 p.m.

The library hours in the evening shall be from 7 to 9:45.

Smoking is permitted on the campus but not in any of the college buildings on the campus.

equal strength with fraternities and "snobbery is rapidly vanishing."

Unfortunately, however, there were "altogether too many" organizations of all types for a college of Washburn's size, the dean continued.

In 1938, a graduating senior, Barbara King, agreed, telling her fellow seniors at a chapel service that perhaps limits should be instituted on activities. She quoted the national officers of two campus sororities, who told her of all the colleges they visited — large and small — Washburn was the most "over-activitied of all."

"Nowhere else, they say, are there so many, many extra-curricular activities in proportion to a comparatively small number of students."

Sometimes other sectors of campus life came under criticism, among them college-sponsored sporting events on Sundays. Occasionally administrators had to fend off complaints that some professors were anti-Bible and even agnostic. In 1932, a Topeka resident complained to President King about the campus visit of a speaker who espoused Communism, but King defended the talk, saying, "Present-day young people demand a right to hear all points of view. They get up in arms if there is any trace of an attitude that they need to be 'protected' from doctrines which may be unsound." Anyway, King said, only three students attended the lecture.

Administrators remained conservative in their views about sex. Letters in King's student discipline file described women who boasted too freely about their exploits with the opposite sex or who drank too heavily, and men who were accused of the same things. In several cases, the students were dismissed or urged to withdraw from school. The mentions were few, so presumably the vast majority of students avoided those deeds — or avoided being discovered.

Dancing the night away, from the 1938 Kaw.

The inevitable arrives

Mostly bad news on the revenue front meant President King fought continually to contain and reduce expenses. In the 1932-1933 academic year, Washburn cut salaries 10 percent. The next year, they were cut 15 percent more. Throughout, Washburn consistently met its payroll, but by mid-1938 the trustees were ordering what President King called "drastic cuts" in positions and salaries. In the 1939-1940 year, expenses had been cut nearly $60,000 below 1931-1932, a reduction of more than 20 percent.

In June 1940, the college dropped its group life and accidental death and dismemberment insurance policies covering faculty and other employees. By then, the effects on morale were showing. The college hired a new law dean in April 1939, and by October 1940 he was offering his resignation to return to the university from which he had come.

In 1938, the college stopped renting space to Washburn High School, saying it faced problems with campus crowding, and President King resigned from the school board. The high school had used the basement of Rice Hall, MacVicar Chapel and some of the science laboratories. While the high school searched for a permanent site, it used other space on campus. In fall 1940, more than two decades after it split from the college, the high school and its 89 students moved off campus to a new space at 19th and Hope streets. In

Thompson's dual 1938 versions: modern, above left, and traditional. Below: as a license plate fixture, 1948.

Ichabod as emblem

Since at least the early 1900s, newspaper writers and yearbook editors had referred to Washburn students, and particularly athletic teams, as sons of Ichabod or daughters of Ichabod — or simply Ichabods.

For the 1938 *Kaw* yearbook, graphic designer Bradbury Thompson took on the task of devising a visual representation for the college. Thompson, who had graduated from Washburn four years earlier, sorted through a myriad of suggestions. Animal images were popular, the kind used by many other colleges. Sketches of various forms of a Jayhawk, the mythical bird used by the University of Kansas, were submitted but, according to the *Kaw* editors, they "so closely paralleled the design of the Kansas Jayhawk that they suggested plagiarism."

Bradbury Thompson, 1934

How about something like Ichabod Crane of Sleepy Hollow fame? The editors thought that idea a false analogy.

Throughout the struggle to devise an emblem, many friends of the college argued that the name was unique and distinctive and ought to have its own representation. After all, "Ichabods" was unique among American colleges.

So Thompson turned to the virtues of Ichabod Washburn himself, the Massachusetts wire maker whose donation caused the college to be named for him. In him, Thompson saw courage and enthusiasm, so he gave the image a "brisk walk." To depict courtesy and a democratic nature, Thompson drew the image tipping his hat and smiling. As for scholarship, the new Ichabod carried a book.

In fact, Thompson produced two Ichabods, one appearing like a mature gentleman of the 1860s, the other more stylized and perhaps modern. The artist was not jealous of his creation, welcoming changes in the appearance of the image so long as any future versions maintained certain essential characteristics: courageous spirit, democratic courtesy, kindness and the studious love of truth.

Since 1938, the Ichabod emblem has appeared as a soldier, a muscled supehero, a bobble-head doll, a license-plate emblem and in various other forms and levels of detail.

1946 it became Washburn Rural High School.

Washburn's annual projected operating deficits mounted, as they had for years: $40,000 in 1937-1938, $41,000 in 1938-1939, $60,000 in 1939-1940. The projected deficits were reduced by onetime gifts totaling $85,000 over those same three years, but even so the college faced a net loss of $56,000 in the period. Even more dismal: By the end of the 1930s net losses were consistently growing.

Looking ahead to the academic and fiscal year ending in June 1941, the operating deficit was projected at $43,000 — equal to roughly $600,000 in 2014 dollars. And the final payment of the principal on the 15-year bonds that financed the late 1920s construction loomed in 1942.

By 1940, it became clear that the red ink could not be sustained, nor could Washburn College in its existing configuration. The administration and the Board of Trustees were faced with the need to act.

By 1940, it became clear that the red ink could not be sustained, nor could Washburn College in its existing configuration. The administration and the Board of Trustees were faced with the need to act.

In May of that year a report by the Chicago accounting firm of Frazer and Torbet recommended to the trustees a thorough reorganization of Washburn and its governance, along with severe cuts in staffing, students and in courses offered. Enrollment, the accountants said, should be limited to about 500 students. The report, which had been commissioned by the trustees, also recommended reducing the number of courses offered, with particular attention to those with small enrollment. According to the accountants, Washburn could reduce courses from more than 1,000 to only 190. Meanwhile, the college should be reorganized into primarily a liberal-arts institution with schools of law and music, but only if the last two supported themselves. The Board of Trustees, the report continued, should be limited to 15 people — over the years, the board had grown to 23 — and each trustee should promise to raise $30,000 a year over his or her five-year term.

Naturally, the administration and faculty considered these proposals drastic, and on June 1, 1940, the trustees formed a committee to make a response. It was headed by King.

Matters were coming to a head. The treasurer's report, made at the same trustees meeting, hinted that drastic measures might be necessary because the college had "no prospect of living within our means" in the upcoming academic year.

King's committee took more than four months to issue its own report. Midway through its work, in early August 1940, King submitted his resignation. Any new plans for the college ought to have the "freest possible development," he wrote, and he did not want to let his own feelings get in the way. Nothing bound him to Washburn; his wife, Zoe Marts King, had died in February of that year.

King's committee finally issued its own report in October 1940, and it took issue with many of the Frazer recommendations. Any reorganization should be evolutionary and handled slowly, the committee said in October 1940, and should be made with an eye to keeping Washburn a high-quality institution. The Frazer study, it said, would reduce Washburn essentially to a "junior-college program" of basic, introductory courses that would be unable to attract even the recommended 500 students.

"No college," King's committee said, "should put its students through an educational 'mill.'"

The joys and foibles of college life, 1939, as seen by a Kaw *staff cartoonist.*

BOWERY BRAWL
CELEBRATION
GOLF
GIMME 'NOTHER SASPARRILA - JOE
WE TEACH GOLF DANCING 25¢
BOB WILSON PASSES BAR EXAMS.
JACK SAVAGE
RESCUE
HOLD TIGHT - HERE I COME
JIM MACKEY
JOHN "SHOTSKY" SHUART RESCUES FOUR PRETTY MAIDS IN DISTRESS
THE ARTHUR MURRAY'S OF WASHBURN - JACK, KENNY, AND BILL.
FIRE
JEAN CAMPBELL
OOOH!! I BEG YOUR PARDON - SO SORRY
LATE
TOPEKA 1051 MI.
BOB SLEDDING ON THE GOLF COURSE
NORVELL IRELAND MISSES BUS AT DES MOINES.
DR. CLITTERHOUSE
GENTLEMEN - THIS CORPSE IS DEAD.
COLLEGIANAS
O-MY-GOSH! WE'RE GONNA CRASH -
AMAZING
ACT 1
TOM MIX AS THE "AMAZING" DR. CLITTERHOUSE
THIS IS PROF. SAXE'S DOBERMANN PINSCHER WATCHING. PROF. SAXE SNAP A PICTURE OF JOE LOGAN WHO IS TAKING A PICTURE OF YOU
LIBRARY
QUIET
AH AH-AH -
BILL DAWSON
TRY LYDIA E. PINKHAM COMPOUND FOR
SHH!
PLEASE BE QUIET
CLICK
CLICK
ROBERT CURRIE

WASHBURN COLLEGE *Bulletin*

June, 1940 • Volume XXV • No. 5

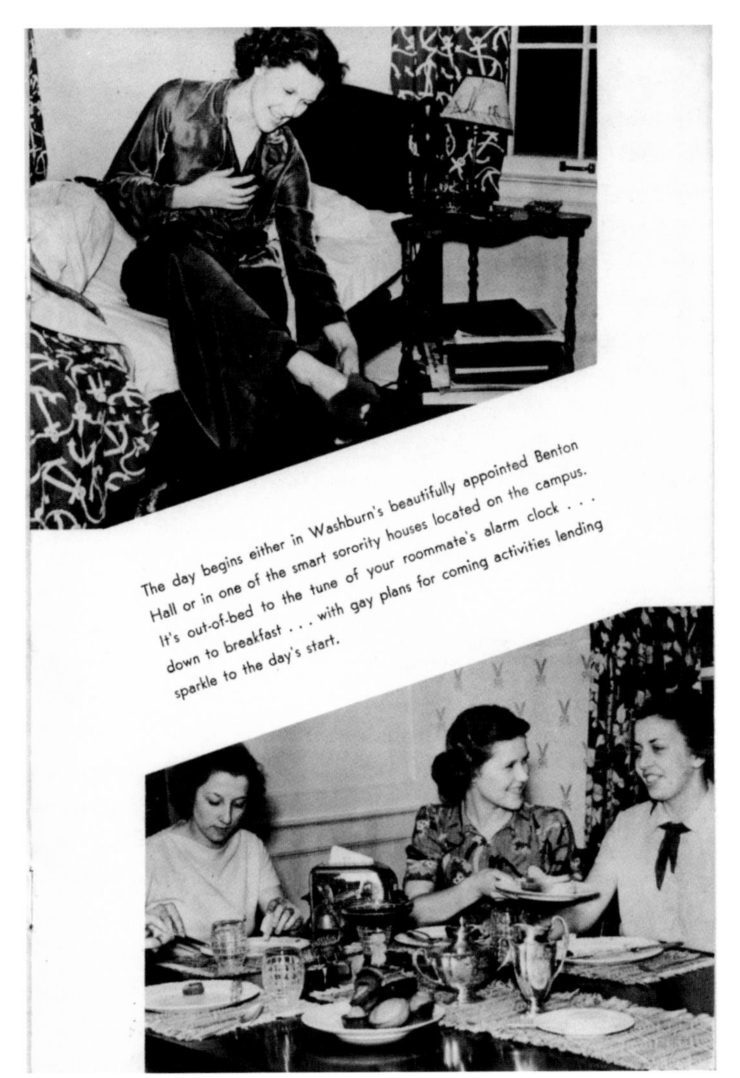

Washburn women and their campus experiences, as depicted by the Bulletin *in 1940.*

Several suggestions presented themselves, and rumors flew. One was to merge with another college — KU? K-State? Emporia? A private college?

The chair of the Board of Trustees, Paul Sweet, said that board members conferred with "more than one" prospect for a consolidation. None of those conversations worked out, he said, in a way that could allow Washburn to pay off its debts.

Other possibilities: Convert Washburn to a junior college. Or move Washburn someplace else. Or cease to exist.

And finally: Turn it over to the taxpayers of Topeka.

A course of action

The decision evolved quickly, and even President King professed surprise at the suddenness of it.

"There had been no suggestion," King later wrote Washburn alumni associations on the East and West Coasts, "that the college was in such a desperate condition."

But King had known something was afoot. In fall 1940 an association of church-related colleges wrote a routine letter to King, seeking Washburn's annual membership dues. King replied that Washburn might not renew.

"Recent, unforeseen developments at Washburn," the president said, "...have made

Washburn's future plans uncertain."

Word was out in the community, as demonstrated by a series of articles published by *The Topeka State Journal* in early November 1940. They described the process by which Fairmount College in Wichita had been taken under the wing of city government in 1926 — influenced by financial problems — and compared the situation with Washburn's. Fairmount, too, had started as a private Congregationalist institution.

Then came what King called a "sudden crystallization" of opinion among the trustees.

The decision was clear and unmistakable. Meeting at the Hotel Jayhawk in downtown Topeka on November 15, 1940, the board voted for Washburn College to close at the end of summer 1941. That would force the issue.

On November 18, King notified the faculty at a special meeting, and said the college faced two courses: becoming a municipal institution or consolidating with another college. The faculty seemed little interested in the latter course.

Where to, now?

Word was out about a big change to come, and Washburn faced immediate problems. Unless something was done, the college would find it impossible to attract students, gain financial support, recruit new faculty or reassure existing faculty and staff. King began writing letters to the presidents of other small colleges; they might soon be seeing applications from Washburn faculty.

"Recent, unforeseen developments at Washburn... have made Washburn's future plans uncertain."

— President King

Amid the hubbub, King agreed with the trustees that he would remain on the job until June 30, 1941, through whatever transition was to come.

The trustees kept working. In December 1940, a committee of the trustees decided to try the path blazed by Fairmount.

The full board accepted the committee recommendation, termed "municipalization," as Washburn's best hope. The effort would require approval first by the Kansas Legislature and then by the voters of Topeka. It would take several months and plenty of energy.

The proposal, based on the same method under which Fairmount had gone municipal, called for Topeka property owners to be taxed an extra two mills to help defray Washburn's costs. The college, its buildings and land would be turned over to a nine-member Board of Regents, four of them nominated by the City Council and four by the Topeka school district. The mayor would become the ninth regent.

As 1941 began, Washburn's backers went to work. Alumni President Pendleton Miller, a Topeka insurance executive, formed a Committee of 100 to promote acceptance of a local property tax to support the college. Petitions were circulated to put the matter on the April 1 ballot. Although businesses would carry the largest tax burden, Miller persuaded them to withhold opposition. He also brought labor unions on board.

From the beginning, sentiment in Topeka appeared to favor the measure, and no group organized to oppose it.

The main questions concerned the value of Washburn property, which the university successfully answered, and the legal methods of transferring it from the Board of Trustees to the new Board of Regents. Washburn's book value — the total of bonds, stock, real estate, mortgage loans and other property listed on its books — totaled a little more than a million dollars. That included acreage in eastern Colorado and in western and southern Kansas, along with 50 farms and 10 residences in Topeka. The Boswell endowment, valued at

President King watched Governor Payne Ratner sign municipal bill, February 7, 1941.

half a million dollars, represented by far the college's largest single asset.

The value of Washburn if all that were sold, or liquidated, was a little more than $800,000. Of course, the idea was not to sell, but to transfer it to a new, taxpayer-supported authority.

The state law allowing Fairmount in Wichita to become a municipal college called for the name of the city to be used for the new institution, and "Fairmount" was lost in that transition. Washburn, however, had plenty of backers who wanted the old name kept, and they went to work altering the legislation. The Legislature acted quickly and on February 6, 1941 — 76 years to the day since the founding of the college — Governor Payne Ratner signed into law a measure enabling not only the vote on becoming a city institution but also retaining the name "Washburn."

In early March, Topeka backers did their part, turning in more than 14,000 signed petitions calling for a city vote. Only 3,500 were required.

And so the future of Washburn was placed on the ballot for April 1, 1941.

Sunday, March 30, 1941 — THE TOPEKA DAILY CAPITAL — 1 C

WILL YOU ACCEPT THIS GIFT?

These and Six Other Buildings and Grounds Will be Given To the City . . . If You Vote YES ☒ for Topeka

Pictured on this page are the buildings and grounds of Washburn College which will become a part of the city school system if the citizens of Topeka vote YES ☒ Tuesday on the question of a Municipal University.

The entire property will be given to the city debt-free. Washburn's debts will be paid from the endowment income or assets. It would cost Topeka at least $1,600,000 today to build these buildings, plus the 160-acre campus.

These buildings will be used to house a Municipal University . . . a part of the public school system of Topeka . . . **which Topeka students may attend at a cost so low that anyone who really wants a college education can get it.**

In addition to these buildings and grounds, the City of Topeka will receive the surplus income from endowment funds . . . the endowment income last year was $32,000.

These buildings and the equipment are adequate to educate a student body nearly twice the size now attending Washburn.

The state law provides that a Municipal University shall be governed by a Board of Regents chosen by your school board and your city commission. The same law limits the taxes for operation of such a university to two mills.

Directly and indirectly, Washburn College is estimated to be **worth more than a MILLION DOLLARS** a year to Topeka.

The loss of Washburn would mean the loss of jobs, of trade, of rent, a loss of population—a dollar-and-cents loss that would be felt by the entire city.

Should the citizens of Topeka not avail themselves of this gift, the college will be closed . . . and the young people of Topeka will either be deprived of a college education or be forced away from home to seek their educational opportunities.

Topeka has had a college for 76 years. Every city in Kansas of 15,000 population has a University, a College or a Junior College. Shall Topeka go forward . . . or go backward 76 years?

It is important that every voter who favors a greater, better Topeka, go to the polls and vote YES ☒ for Topeka.

Vote YES ☒ for Topeka

This advertisement paid for by friends of Municipal University Plan.

WHITING ATHLETIC FIELD HOUSE

BENTON HALL, GIRLS DORMITORY

ZENAS CRANE OBSERVATORY

CARNEGIE LIBRARY

MULVANE ART MUSEUM

THOMAS GYMNASIUM FOR GIRLS

BOSWELL LAW SCHOOL BLDG.

RICE HALL OF SCIENCE

MacVICAR SCHOOL OF MUSIC

Vote YES ☒ for Topeka

Shortly before the election, backers of municipalization placed this advertisement asking, "Shall Topeka go forward...or go backward 76 years?"

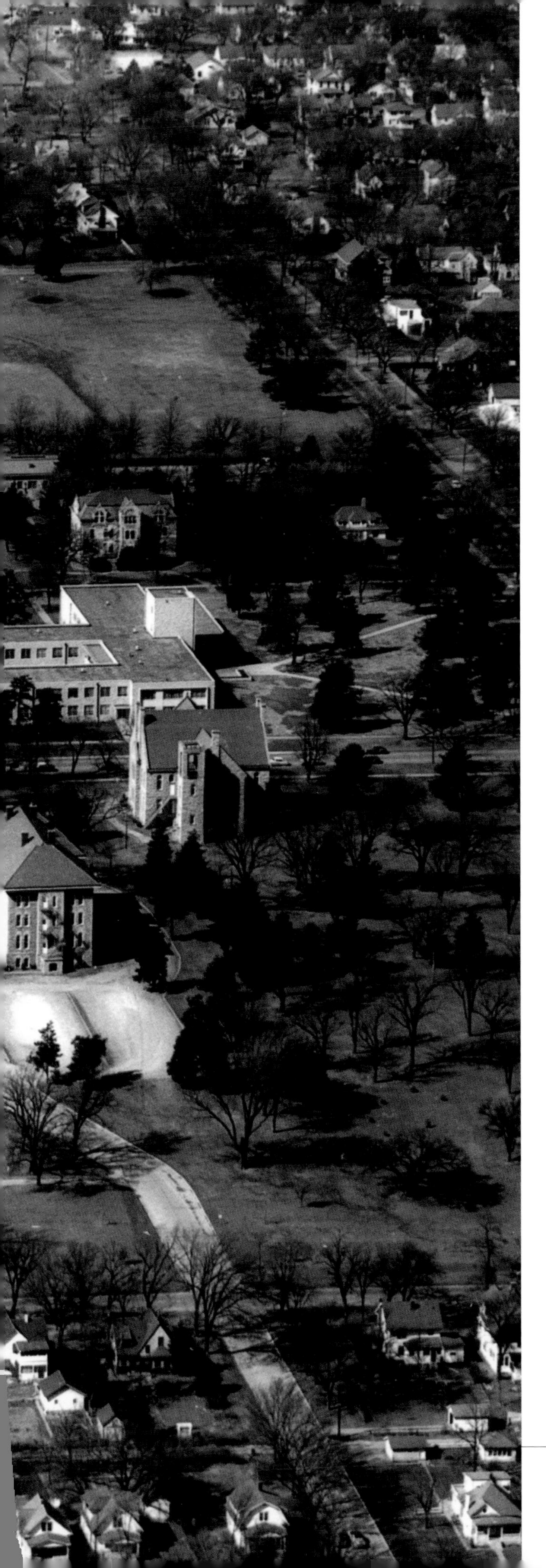

The Municipal Way

Four blasts from the big whistle at Beatrice Creamery downtown signaled the news to Topeka:

Washburn and the city now were joined. The college was saved. It would become Washburn Municipal University of Topeka.

By a nearly 4-to-1 ratio — 17,825 "yes" votes to only 4,481 "no" — the voters of Topeka on April 1, 1941, approved the "municipalization" of the private college. The city's property-tax payers would support its operations, joining students paying their tuition and donors giving to the endowment.

Carloads of Washburn students patrolled downtown Topeka, hollering in celebration.

Phillip King, his work done, resigned as president immediately afterward and on April 24, Arthur G. Sellen, dean of the College of Arts and Sciences, was named acting president.

On June 9, 1941, the Washburn Board of Trustees, after more than three-quarters of a century of running the institution, formally turned it over to the newly appointed nine-member Washburn Board of Regents. Paul B. Sweet, chairman of the trustees, presented a copy of

Numbers

Washburn enrollment

» 1941	700
» 1960	3,030

Topeka population

» 1940	67,833
» 1960	119,484

Now "municipalized," Washburn in the 1950s.

Washburn Review

VOL. 58 — TOPEKA, KANSAS, FRIDAY, APRIL 4, 1941 — No. 23

Municipal Issue Through With 4 To 1 Margin

Topeka Voters Take Over Three Million Dollar Gift

Appointing Board of Regents Next Step in Reorganization

Washburn's future became assured last Tuesday when the citizens of Topeka voted by an overwhelming majority to make the school a municipal university. The complete but unofficial vote showed 17,825 for the proposition and 4,481 against.

The next step in the municipalization of the new university now that the voters have given the "go" sign, will be the appointment of a board of regents. The new board will be composed of nine members. Four will be appointed by the board of education, and four by the city commission. The mayor, newly elected Frank J. Warren, will serve ex-officio as the ninth member. The city commission takes office next Tuesday, and the appointments are expected by the end of next week.

'Outward Bound' Ready For Stage In Record Time

Curtain Rises At 8:15 O'Clock On Popular Dramatic Fantasy

Spring Vacation Starts Thursday

Easter vacation will start at 8:00 next Thursday morning, April 10, and will end with the resumption of classes the following Tuesday morning, April 15, Dr. Philip C. King, president has announced.

Pendleton Miller, head of Committee of 100 during successful college campaign.

Seniors Take Next Chapel Spotlight

Dr. King Addresses Annual Assembly

Music Groups Plan Recital

Include Soloists In Annual Program

Gala Midnight Rally Proves Ichabods' Joy Over Election

1941-1966

1941: Topeka voters approved a property tax to support Washburn.
1942: Spring. Student Council included a representative from Washburn black students.
— Law School admission requirements were tightened. Entering students were required to have a bachelor's or equivalent degree, up from the previously required 90 hours of college credit.
1946: A Washburn music professor, Everett Fetter, founded the Topeka Symphony Orchestra, which played in MacVicar Chapel its first 10 years.
—University Place opened to house student and faculty veterans and their families. It became known as "diaper row."
1949: Law School enrollment reached nearly 300 and the graduating class of lawyers totaled 80.
1952-53: A planetarium was installed in Crane Observatory.
1955: Morgan Hall opened.
1956: Law School moved out of Boswell and into a remodeled Carnegie.
— Holbrook Hall was razed.
1957: On October 16, Parley Womer died.

the deed to the 160-acre campus to Arthur J. Carruth, chair of the new Board of Regents. The board agreed to maintain Washburn as a liberal arts college in perpetuity.

"By the grace of the voters of Topeka," Carruth said, "we are here today in celebration of the birth of a university rather than in mourning of the death of a college. The university's major financial troubles are over."

The old Board of Trustees continued to exist as administrator of the endowment. That act made the Washburn College Board of Trustees the university's basic fund-raising body, and they would keep the name for decades to come.

There was other good news beyond the results of the vote. Washburn's deficit at the end of the 1940-1941 academic year — projected in 1940 at up to $43,000 — amounted instead to about $23,000. Most of the difference came from tens of thousands of dollars in spending cuts from the original budget, cuts made in November 1940 as the trustees were deciding whether to close the school. Even with that, the deficit was the second largest of the preceding four years.

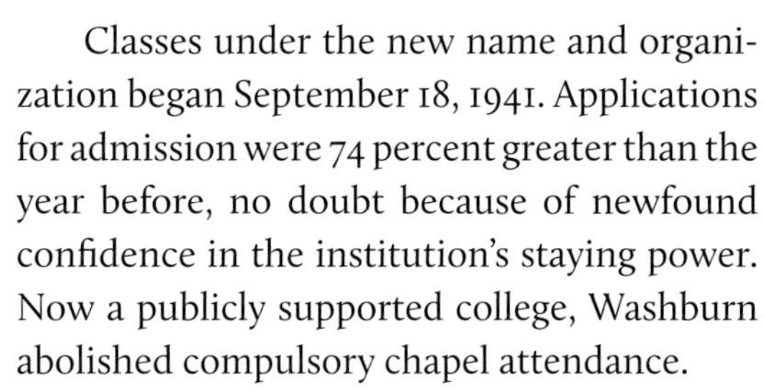

Classes under the new name and organization began September 18, 1941. Applications for admission were 74 percent greater than the year before, no doubt because of newfound confidence in the institution's staying power. Now a publicly supported college, Washburn abolished compulsory chapel attendance.

By June 1942, the tax paid by Topeka property owners generated more than $133,000 for Washburn — the kind of financial support that would have been considered a miracle only two years before.

The transformation worked as expected. But there would be no settling into routine. Less than three months after the opening of fall classes, Japanese aircraft bombed Pearl Harbor and the United States went to war. The newly reconstituted Washburn would send many of its students into the military and many of its graduates into professions aiding the war effort, and would transform its campus into a training ground.

Gradually consumed

Looking back at the turbulent 1941-1942 school year, the *Kaw* yearbook noted that, in some ways, college life had gone on unobstructed despite the war.

Mixers, open houses, formals, homecoming parades, celebrations after football victories, campus romances — all remained a part of college life. Women joined the Splash Club for swimming and diving, the Ichadettes pep

1960: The *Washburn Law Journal* published its first issues.
— Washburn began offering a master's degree in teacher education.
— Philip King, president of Washburn in the 1930s, died in December in New York City.
1961: Washburn began receiving financial aid from the State of Kansas.
— Possibly because of extensive installation of air conditioning, summer enrollment rose 30 percent over the year before.
— Whiting Field House was remodeled.
1962: The "White House," home of Washburn presidents and their families since it was constructed in 1903, was demolished. A house at 1626 Jewell was made the new residence until 1971, when the president moved to 3130 Shadow Lane.
1963: IBM 1620 computer was purchased for the university.
1964: The Municipal University of Wichita became part of the Kansas state system, leaving Washburn as the only municipal university in Kansas, and one of the few in the United States.
1965: February 6. Centennial of Washburn's founding.
— John Henderson became president.
— KTWU went on the air in October.

group, the Archery Club, or Orchesis, a dance club. Men had the Theolog Club, a mostly religious discussion group covering unlimited topics, along with multiple sports. For both sexes there were the Quill Club for creative writers, the Press Club for student journalists and the Sketch Club for artists. Also, there were the band, orchestra, choirs and the drama club.

The yearbook acknowledged, however, that the war had brought some new things.

"We are here today in celebration of the birth of a university rather than in mourning the death of a college."

— *Arthur J. Carruth, Board of Regents*

In early 1942, Washburn adopted a plan to accelerate graduation. Classes would go year-round, broken into three semesters, with brief vacations and no long holiday periods. A student who attended continuously could graduate in less than three years.

Many Washburn students already took life seriously. The *Kaw* estimated that 65 percent of students held part-time jobs in offices, stores, restaurants, packinghouses and service stations, along with filling many clerical positions with the State of Kansas.

By summer 1942, the demands of war made things more serious. Because of the draft or their own choice, students began departing to serve in the military or to work in war-related industries. The Law School, filled with young men who had no draft deferment, lost much of its enrollment and the law fraternity, Phi Alpha Delta, went inactive. Wartime research boosted the demand for classes in mathematics, chemistry and physics. To meet the new demand for office workers, Washburn for the first time offered shorthand and typing to freshmen.

New military training programs sprouted, and so did uniforms on campus. Soon after the United States entered the war, Washburn became a pilot training site for the Navy V-5 program. By the war's end, 900 aviators would receive ground and flight training.

War bond drives raised thousands of dollars from faculty and employees.

A new leader

Arthur Sellen's term as acting president came to an end in May 1942, and the *Kaw* saluted his effort, which had carried Washburn

Behind a row of batteries, Navy cadets studied at Washburn.

through its transformation to public institution and through the U.S. declaration of war.

"Truly Washburn's man of the year," the student editors wrote, "in his quiet, capable leadership through Washburn's difficult period of change." Sellen returned to his old post as dean of arts and sciences.

Bryan S. Stoffer

On June 1, 1942, Bryan S. Stoffer stepped into the president's job. His resume bore strong religious credentials and thus resembled that of his predecessors, even though Stoffer's Washburn was no longer denominational.

Stoffer, who was in his mid-40s, held degrees in divinity and philosophy, and as an ordained minister had been pastor of three churches in Ohio. He and his wife later lived and taught in India. In the five years before his arrival at Washburn he had been president of Doane College in Crete, Nebraska, southwest of Lincoln. Like Washburn, Doane was founded by New England Congregationalists. Charles Boswell, a big Washburn benefactor, had left another slice of his estate to Doane.

Friends described Stoffer's manner as unruffled and hard-working. At the top of his agenda was the war.

In July 1942, Washburn's part-time Civilian Pilot Training program was made full-time. The program, begun three years earlier, was paid for by the federal government and supervised by the Navy. It trained and funneled pilot candidates into the military. Benton Hall was used to house the program and its participants.

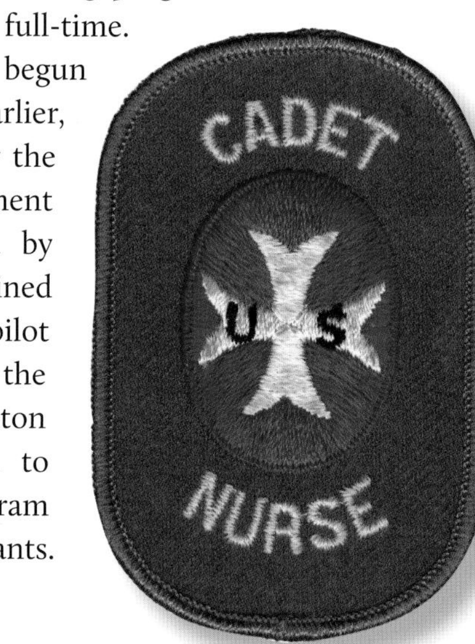

Benton was temporarily renamed "Yorktown Hall" after the Navy aircraft carrier that itself was named for the place where the British surrendered, ending the American Revolution.

Aviation students rode buses to the Topeka airport for their hands-on work. Hundreds of pilots got basic instruction through the program, and in the first full year alone the university made more than $180,000 from hosting it.

The Naval Reserve took over sorority houses, and suddenly scores of Navy uniforms appeared on campus, a signal of the beginning of the Navy V-7 plan, under which juniors and seniors could enlist in the Navy reserve and still finish school. Afterward, they would go to midshipmen's schools and become commissioned ensigns in the reserve.

In July 1943, the Navy organized a V-12 officer training unit at Washburn. Candidates attended class with regular students and participated in athletics. As active-duty personnel, they also were subject to military discipline and wore uniforms on campus. The program was opened to African-American candidates. Among V-12 graduates was the future syndicated political columnist Carl Rowan.

"Each succeeding month," the *Kaw* noted in 1943, "has meant the end of college for the duration to a growing number of Washburn men." The yearbook was dedicated "to the Ichabods, students of today — soldiers of tomorrow."

On a campus filled with men in Navy blues, the *Kaw* one year later acknowledged the dramatic difference: "The effects of total war have changed it from a peacetime institution to one expending its every effort in the war crisis."

Even sorority houses got new names. Zeta Tau Alpha moved out of its house, which was renamed "Halsey Hall." William Frederick Halsey was an aggressive Navy admiral who commanded the Pacific fleet. Alpha Phi members also moved off campus and turned their house over to Navy personnel. It was renamed "Enterprise" hall, the same as a long line of American warships, the latest of which was an aircraft carrier fighting in the Pacific. The Delta Gamma sorority house was converted to a dispensary.

Eventually, all campus housing was claimed for military use.

Among fraternities, Phi Delta Theta membership showed the effects of the wartime call-up. Dramatically reduced in numbers, only 15 members were pictured in the yearbook. Nine wore Navy blues for their portraits.

In March 1945, in the final months of war, the United States established a Cadet Nurse Corps and scores of nurses were trained at Washburn before the war ended later that year.

In the last academic year of the war, total enrollment barely reached 1,100. The change over three-plus years was striking.

The Navy gave Washburn a plaque to mark its participation in the V-5 program and its successor, the V-12 program.

With peace, new challenges

As quickly as war transformed the campus, the coming of peace would transform it even faster. With the surrender of Germany in May 1945 and Japan that September, the number of uniforms seen on campus quickly dwindled and within months, Navy training programs shut down. In all, more than 2,400 Washburn students and former students served in the military. Sixty-seven of those died.

Washburn was about to face a new challenge — dealing with a peacetime, postwar flood of returning veterans.

Carl Rowan, who became a nationally syndicated columnist and author, took Navy training at Washburn in World War II and became one of the Navy's first African-American officers.

By the late 1940s, President Stoffer said in his annual report, veterans constituted half of all Washburn students. With their maturity, experience and motivation, he said, they had strengthened the campus.

None was more motivated than a 26-year-old veteran of the Allied invasion of Italy who in fall 1949 enrolled at Washburn, seeking to finish work toward a bachelor's degree he began at the University of Kansas and to earn a law degree. He was Robert J. Dole, who grew up in Russell, Kansas, and attended the University of Kansas before being called to active duty in 1943. In 1945, he was severely injured in combat and lost the use of his right hand. Afterward, he married a woman who had helped nursed him back to health. He spent one year at the University of Arizona and now aimed to get both degrees.

Robert Dole, from 1951 Kaw.

Doing so would not prove easy. A natural right-hander, Dole found it difficult to take notes with his left hand and had to bring a bulky recording device with him to class. At night, he painfully transcribed the notes. Through it all, he persevered. At exam time, which required filling bluebooks with handwritten answers, he made a special arrangement with professors to outline his thoughts. He passed with flying colors. In June 1952, Dole graduated magna cum laude. Already, he had won election to the Kansas Legislature.

The GI Bill made it possible for more Americans than ever to get a college education. Within four months of the Japanese surrender in September 1945, Washburn recorded 170 students — about one in 10 of all students — who were enrolled under the GI Bill. A little more than a year later, in spring 1947, the number of veterans reached 976.

Veterans had experienced much in the war, and naturally they showed more maturity than others who had not served. Like Dole, having lost years of their youth, they were eager to get on with college and with life.

Not only were veterans — whether newcomers to Washburn or returnees — older than traditional college age, they also were more likely to be married and not likely to be living with parents. Housing them became an immediate problem and it was alleviated somewhat by construction of frame apartments hastily built east of Moore Bowl and south of Whiting. Formally called University Place, the new buildings were open to student and faculty veterans with families. So began Washburn's own marker of the Baby Boom, and the project soon received the nickname "Diaper Row."

With their return, Washburn rebuilt its enrollment and soon hit new highs. By the 1948-1949 academic year, total enrollment shot past 2,000, nearly double what it had been in the last year of the war. Two hundred twenty-six of those were in the Law School, compared with only 78 four years earlier.

Sororities and fraternities began to restock their memberships. In the fall semester of 1945, just as Japan surrendered, Kappa Sigma fraternity numbered only six active members. By spring 1946, its membership ballooned to 40.

Military education returned in June 1948 — not with the Navy but with the newest branch of the military, the U.S. Air Force, created the year before. Washburn established an Air Force Reserve Officers Training Corps Unit, headed by two Air Force officers. The ROTC unit shared a frame building, which had been moved from the Lake City Ordnance Plant east of Kansas City to the west side of Moore Bowl, with art department kilns and with engineering classrooms.

Postwar campus life

Some old customs hung on and one was revived. Reminiscent of the turn-of-the century Washburn Campus Improvement Association, in spring 1946 the university dismissed classes for Dandelion Day, in which students were expected to dig up the weeds that were overrunning campus. The *Kaw* yearbook showed some students attacking the weeds vigorously by hand or with hoes, while others languidly took the chance to relax on the lawns.

A dandelion queen was chosen that year, along with the traditional homecoming queen, a snow queen and a queen for the day. Sororities and fraternities renewed their annual parties and dances as they worked to rebuild their rosters.

Each year since 1937, Washburn staged a student-faculty reception, which took place in September or October. In 1955, the name would be changed from "reception" to "mixer." Punch and sherbet were served and entertainment was provided by a ventriloquist and a five-piece dance band. Eventually the custom would be dropped.

The Student Council faced questions that ranged from symbolic to quite real.

As for symbols, in May 1948 the council

A clothier chose three students to model the latest in 1947 campus wear, top. Bottom: Kicking back in the snack bar, 1949.

Following pages: Dancing the night away at a late 1940s event called a "varsity."

adopted the Ichabod as official emblem of the student body. As for thornier matters, in October 1949, the Student Council faced a problem that represented a beginning stage of the Civil Rights era.

The popular Meadow Acres Ballroom had been scheduled for that fall's homecoming dance, but the proprietors announced they would exclude black participants. The dance was scheduled for a Saturday night, when the ballroom also was open to the public, and the operators worried that white customers might be reluctant to dance in the same room as African-Americans. The Student Council moved the homecoming dance to campus.

In 1951, a Hobo King and Queen "reigned" over the homecoming parade. Winners were selected from costumed candidates who were judged on the steps of the library. The parade itself went along Kansas Avenue. Twenty floats, several bands and several political campaigners took part. The Hobo King and Queen were joined by four candidates for homecoming queen, who would be announced at halftime of the football game against St. Benedict's.

One tradition dating only to 1941 — the name of the school — underwent yet another change in hopes of improving its recognition. On June 1, 1952, the Board of Regents removed "Municipal" and shortened the name to Washburn University of Topeka.

Right, Veterans housing in the late 1940s

Arthur Allen "Art" Fletcher, a football star at Washburn and later a player in the National Football League, went on to advise four U.S. presidents and to serve as a delegate to the United Nations. As executive secretary of the United Negro College Fund, he was said to have created the phrase, "a mind is a terrible thing to waste." Fletcher, a member of the Washburn Athletic Hall of Fame and recipient of the Alumni Distinguished Service award and an honorary doctorate, briefly considered running for the 1996 GOP nomination for president.

Additions to campus

Shortly after the end of World War II, Shawnee County decided that the Washburn campus would be a suitable place for a war memorial. Washburn students took up the idea, and proposed that the memorial be in the form of a student union. In May 1946, hundreds of them signed a petition and pledged to pay a fee of $3 a semester to help build it.

Alumni, friends and public school children pitched in on a $250,000 fundraising campaign that began in 1947. The combined contributions made the idea real and fully paid for the new building. The Memorial Student Union opened December 3, 1951. A Sadie Hawkins dance — in which women did the inviting — was the first event.

A bronze plaque was dedicated on Washburn Day, February 6, 1952, honoring Washburn students and Shawnee Countians who gave their lives not only in World War II, but also in World War I and in the Korean War, which had begun in mid-1950.

As the campaign for the new union was still under way, the idea arose for a new administration building. In 1947, Harrison S. Morgan — who had been a trustee of Washburn for a decade and a half — gave the university $200,000 to help build the structure and later added $200,000 more. After Morgan's death in May 1953, his estate contributed stocks valued in 1954 at more than $600,000. The structure, which would also house the university library and class-

The Memorial Union opened in 1951. Inside, a plaque installed in 1952 listed names of students and Shawnee County residents who died in the world wars and the Korean conflict.

Beanie-wearing men cleaned the Washburn crest in the floor at Morgan Hall in 1958.

rooms, would be named Morgan Hall, after the donor's late wife, Margaret Mulvane Morgan. The family was accustomed to supporting Washburn; Margaret Morgan's father was Joab Mulvane, the Topeka businessman and civic leader who in 1922 gave Washburn $50,000 for the Mulvane Art Museum.

Planning for Morgan Hall began in 1951, ground was broken in 1954 and it opened in 1955. Final cost was $1 million. One sign of the times came two years later, when Morgan was equipped with air conditioning. With the move of the library to Morgan, Carnegie was remodeled for the Law School. It was dedicated to its new use in February 1956.

The Union and Morgan Hall were only the beginning of a postwar building program. In late 1952 Stoffer laid out plans for a new science building and a new auditorium and music building. Forecasts were for enrollment to grow into the 1960s, meaning there would be increased demand for services and space.

Once veterans began to graduate and move on to careers, Washburn's total enrollment settled back in the vicinity of 1,500 for the first half of the 1950s. In 1955, it began a steady rise, passing 2,000 in 1956 and exceeding 3,000 in 1960.

Right, above: Carruth men's dormitory. Below: married students housing.

Facing page: conversations aplenty on the crowded steps of Carnegie, 1951, as displayed in opening pages of the Kaw *yearbook.*

A demanding future

By 1956, faculty departures added to the worries of administrators. Too many members of the faculty, Stoffer reported, were being hired away by private businesses, which could offer higher salaries. Meanwhile, fewer potential faculty members were coming out of graduate schools. To make teaching salaries more attractive, he said, the school's endowment needed boosting.

Meanwhile, more students began to attend at non-traditional times. Night school enrollment showed surprising increases, driven both by Topekans older than the traditional college age and by college-age students whose jobs made attending difficult during weekdays.

Stoffer pointed to the oncoming legions of college-age Americans that would result from the postwar Baby Boom. They would begin flocking to campuses in the ensuing 10 years, he said in 1956, and Washburn would need resources to meet the need. Stoffer

social activities [illegible] for you just [illegible] hope that in the years to co[illegible] this book will be a [illegible] rem[illegible] years s[illegible] at W[illegible] and [illegible] that you [illegible]

Better days on the field and on the court

After muddling through the war years with constantly changing rosters and losing records, the Washburn football team after the war began to improve, starting in 1946 under Coach Dick Godlove. In 1949 the Ichabods won seven games and shared the championship of the Central Intercollegiate Conference. They lost only to Northern Illinois and Emporia State. The Ichabods had joined the CIC in 1941 after departing the Missouri Valley Conference.

More co-championships came under Godlove in 1953, when Washburn lost only to Fort Hays State, and 1954, when the Ichabods fell again to Fort Hays State and also to Nebraska Omaha. Godlove remained coach through the 1958 season.

In 1964, under third-year coach Ellis Rainsburger, the Ichabods won their first outright conference title since 1930 with an overall record of eight victories and only one defeat. The loss came to Nebraska-Kearney. Two players were named to the Associated Press Little All-America squad, running back Bob Hardy and lineman Dode Lesser.

Basketball at Whiting in 1962.

The postwar basketball Ichabods also improved, posting winning records most years and winning CIC championships in 1950-1951 under coach Adrian Miller and 1951-1952 under Marion McDonald.

Homecoming 1958: above left, queen candidates bedecked with flowers from Hawaiian alumnus Meyer Ueoka. Above right, house decorations.
In 1960, football players ran onto the field while cheerleaders applauded.

The 1965 alumni homecoming dance at the Shawnee County fairgrounds, above. Below left, building a float in 1962; right, smartly dressed football crowd of the 1960s.

A little more than nine months after Science Hall was dedicated, President Bryan Stoffer, right, died. In 1961, the building was renamed for him, above.

turned to the Kansas Legislature, asking it to supplement the tax contributions made by Topekans, who in 1952 paid a little more than half of the university's operating income. The campaign for state aid would require several years, but in 1961 it would succeed.

Washburn kept on growing. In May 1958, a 48-unit building to house married students opened in the southeast corner of campus. Early the next year, in the northwest corner of campus, a new residence hall for men was opened. It was named for Arthur J. Carruth, chairman of the Board of Regents.

Washburn would need the new space. In 1959, total enrollment approached 3,000, and more than 1,300 of those registered for at least some night classes.

On September 19, 1960, Stoffer's 18th year as president of the university, Science Hall was dedicated. It housed departments of astronomy, biology, chemistry, physics, engineering and home economics. The university telescope was moved to the new hall from its longtime home in Crane Observatory.

Barely two weeks after the dedication ceremony, on October 4, Stoffer left his office for the hospital. He was suffering from myasthenia gravis, a muscle weakness that affected his eyelids and his respiratory, throat and speech muscles. He had noticed the symptoms for two years.

On March 19, 1961, Bryan Stoffer died. He was 64. On June 4 the new Science Hall was named after him.

Stoffer left a physical legacy of several new buildings and a financial legacy of an endowment that had quintupled in his 18 years, from $1 million to $5 million. When he assumed the presidency of the newly public college in 1941, enrollment was 700. When he died, it had topped 3,000.

The Review called him the university's "old friend and senior adviser."

A new world

The year he died brought success for Stoffer's drive for financial help from the State of Kansas. The Legislature authorized $3 per credit hour in which freshmen and sophomores were enrolled, the idea being that the aid would reduce pressures on state colleges and universities for those two years of education. However, no matter how much or how little Washburn spent on juniors, seniors,

Stoffer's successor, Harold Sponberg, above. He was inaugurated in 1962 in ceremonies at Whiting Field House, left.

law students and others, the total would not change. Admittedly limited, the financial help was a start, and generated $180,000 in its first year.

The regents named Arthur F. Engelbert, dean of the College, as acting president and set out to find a permanent president. Their wish list called for a Ph.D.-holder, 40 to 50 years old, who was proven in an academic setting as an administrator and teacher.

The man they found had those characteristics. Harold Sponberg was 42 years old when he accepted Washburn's offer in July 1961. He studied psychology and rhetoric at the University of Minnesota, and in 1952 received a Ph.D. from Michigan State University. He came to Washburn from a job as first vice president at Northern Michigan College. He was a native Minnesotan, raised on a farm. He had graduated from Gustavus Adolphus College, where he played guard on the football team and won all-conference honors.

Sponberg was only the second president of Washburn who was not an ordained minister — after George Herrick in the late 1890s. He took office January 1, 1962, inheriting a university with a $2 million annual budget.

That October, Sponberg was inaugurated with considerable ceremony. Just before the event, Arthur J. Carruth, who had headed the regents for their entire existence, died. With

"Unless the university relates itself to the demands for liberally educated people with know-how, we will be lost in the jet wash of the new age. We will be wandering aimlessly in the tomorrows."

— Harold Sponberg

Stoffer's and now Carruth's deaths, the two men who had led the university since before World War II were gone from the scene. Carruth's death happened too late to remove his

Louis Armstrong entertained at the All-School Party, March 11, 1960.

name from the inauguration program.

In Sponberg's address, the new president acknowledged three of his predecessors — Peter McVicar, Parley Womer and Bryan Stoffer. Then he turned to the present and the future. He talked of living in a time of "breathless change" for America and the world. He pointed to the space flights of the Soviet Union's Yuri Gagarin and the U.S. astronaut John Glenn, and the launching of the Telstar communications satellite.

"Unless the university relates itself to the demands for liberally educated people with know-how," he said, "we will be lost in the jet wash of the new age. We will be wandering aimlessly in the tomorrows."

Looking to the university's 100th anniversary three years down the road in 1965, Sponberg also called for establishment of a fund to mark Washburn's centennial.

From the first, Harold Sponberg proved to be a go-getter. A newspaper reporter described him as someone "who could make a half-hour speech at a bus stop — and be cheered when he finished."

"The spirit and the support is here," he told another reporter, "to make Washburn a truly fine university in the Middle West. I've never seen such potential for a university of this type."

His task was to improve the image of Washburn and, measured in money at least, he succeeded. In three years, the endowment rose from $5.6 million to $8 million. The Kansas Legislature broadened its support, now counting credit hours carried by juniors and seniors as well as those carried by underclassmen in its contribution. By mid-1964, Sponberg reported that the university was financially healthy, its balance sheets firmly in the black.

Total enrollment of undergraduate, graduate and law students, which hit 3,800 in Sponberg's first year, 1962, passed 4,000 in 1964 on the way to almost 4,500 in 1965.

In summer 1963, Sponberg held the first meetings aimed at establishing a university television station.

The Centennial Fund, meanwhile, reached more than $1.2 million by the school's 100th year.

Sponberg showed some David-vs.-Goliath spirit when Washburn's debate team was invited for the first time to the Heart of America debate tournament at the University of Kansas. KU, Sponberg remarked, "had never deigned to invite Washburn."

Was Washburn good enough? Evidently so; the Ichabods won the tournament and continued as a powerhouse in debate.

Times they were a-changin'

As the first children of the Baby Boom reached college age, signs appeared in popular culture that the new and massive generation would have to be served. Entertainment, beginning with folk music and its legacy of protest and evolving into spirited and defiant forms of rock 'n' roll, focused increasingly on the Boomers.

In 1964, the College Concert series

Brown vs. Board — the Washburn connection

Charles Scott

John Scott

Charles Bledsoe

Elisha Scott

Lester Goodell

George Brewster

Harold Fatzer

Delmas Hill

When the U.S. Supreme Court struck down school desegregation in 1954, Washburn graduates played important roles on both sides of the issue.

Legal challenges to "separate-but-equal" schools, which separated students by race but often were unequal in quality, had come to the high court from four states — South Carolina, Virginia, Delaware and Kansas — and from the District of Columbia. They were consolidated under the name of the Kansas case, *Brown vs. Board of Education of Topeka*.

Brown was filed on February 28, 1951, in U.S. District Court in Topeka by three African-American Washburn graduates who worked with the local branch of the National Association for the Advancement of Colored People. Charles Scott, John Scott and Charles Bledsoe — members of a Topeka firm headed by 1916 Washburn law graduate Elisha Scott — filed the lawsuit. At trial, they joined with two NAACP lawyers to argue the case.

The lawyers for the school board, Lester Goodell and George Brewster, and for the state, Harold Fatzer, also graduated from Washburn law, as had one member of the three-judge panel, Delmas Hill.

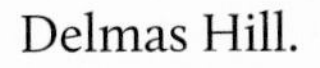

The plaintiffs lost at the district-court level, and then took the case to the Supreme Court. At that level, another Washburn graduate, Assistant Attorney General Paul Wilson, represented the state. He received research help from a Washburn professor, Jim Ahrens, and two other graduates, Peter Caldwell and Charles McCarter.

Paul Wilson

Peter Caldwell

In 1984, a statue commemorating the decision, entitled "Common Justice," was placed in the lobby of the Law School Building.

brought to Washburn the New Christy Minstrels, a popular and non-political group, but it also brought a group featuring Bob Gibson, who had worked with some of the politically active folk-singers of the 1950s and 1960s, and the Smothers Brothers, the folk satirists whose comedy contained a political edge. Students heard John Howard Griffin, a white man who disguised himself as black to experience what it was like to be African-American in the Deep South and wrote about it in *Black Like Me*. And the civil rights theme was furthered by the appearance of comedian and activist Dick Gregory.

Offstage, too, the university faced the new era.

Washburn listed among its alumni several of the lawyers who had argued the case of *Brown vs. Board of Education*, so the school was no stranger to the civil rights era. Unlike local public schools, Washburn had accepted black students from its beginning after the

Civil War.

In 1960, an interracial group of 14 students picketed a downtown Topeka dime store that was part of a group of stores that had segregated lunch counters in the South

As the civil-rights struggle broadened, the university found itself bumping up against rising expectations. In 1964, the campus chapter of the National Association for the Advancement of Colored People complained that some off-campus landlords refused to rent to minorities. The NAACP chapter asked that any landlord listed by the university as providing student housing sign a non-discrimination pledge, and that the dean of students investigate allegations of discrimination. Sponberg replied mildly, requesting non-conforming landlords "not ask to be listed."

Entertainment, beginning with folk music and its legacy of protest and evolving into spirited and defiant forms of rock 'n' roll, focused increasingly on the new and massive generation.

A seal for Washburn's Centennial.

Centennial — and a new leader

As 1964 turned to 1965, Sponberg finished his third year in office. Two weeks later, in mid-January 1965, he announced he would be leaving in June for Eastern Michigan University in Ypsilanti. As it happened, the university probably should not have been surprised at his brief tenure.

Evidently, Sponberg had begun looking for a different job only a few months after his inauguration. His personnel file in the Washburn archives contains a letter from the president of a state college in New York, dated April 1963, promising to review his credentials and saying his application should receive considerable support.

The yearlong celebration of Washburn's 100th anniversary went on as scheduled, beginning with a convocation on Founders' Day, February 6, 1965, which was broadcast on Topeka radio and television. The next day Kansas historian Emory Lindquist gave a speech entitled "Washburn University and the Tradition of Civility."

Centennial events culminated in October 1965. Nineteen former homecoming queens returned to campus to celebrate the institution's 100th year. Featured were a bonfire, pep rallies and what was called the largest homecoming parade in school history. That same month, Washburn's own television station, KTWU, went on the air.

And in the middle of it all, Washburn's new president was inaugurated.

John Henderson had been president at Iowa Wesleyan College and before that dean of students at Western Illinois University. Like Sponberg, he had moved up rapidly, having taken the Iowa Wesleyan job only in March 1963.

Unlike Sponberg, Henderson kept his swearing-in at MacVicar Chapel modest. The printed program barely amounted to a pamphlet, in sharp contrast with Sponberg's production three years earlier. Henderson said he hoped the simple nature of the ceremony would symbolize that much remained to be done — and that Washburn's resources were limited.

Henderson took a more modest approach than his predecessor.

"We have no vision of quantitative bigness," Henderson said in his inaugural message. "Nor are we asking for Washburn to be all things to all people."

A report that same year by an accrediting team put his remarks in context. The accreditors noted that Washburn was "discomfited as it sees increasing numbers of students dissipate the limited resources" available from Topeka taxpayers and the endowment fund.

In years to come, the accreditors said,

Washburn on the air

In July 1963, representatives from the Menninger and Garvey foundations, the Kansas Association of School Boards and the Kansas Department of Public Instruction met with Washburn representatives at a Topeka restaurant. Their topic: Establishing an educational television station.

The idea had been around. In fact, the Federal Communications Commission had allocated one television channel to the University of Kansas and another to Kansas State for just such a project. But the Legislature turned down the idea of a state educational TV authority, and neither university went forward with the concept. A study by broadcasters and legal experts devised a new plan to reallocate the two channels to cover more of the Kansas population, putting the easternmost channel in Topeka.

About that time, executives of Stauffer Publications' Topeka television station, WIBW, decided to move their transmitter west, farther from the signal of Kansas City stations. They approached KU, K-State and Washburn officials, offering their old equipment.

Washburn jumped at the idea, seeing the possibility of broadcasting classroom lectures to public schools in the state. Ownership of WIBW's old tower was transferred to Washburn and the university purchased some of the station's old equipment.

The university asked for support from area school districts — based on a per-student fee — and from other colleges, from charitable groups and from various levels of government.

By January 1964, the Garvey Foundation had offered $25,000 to help, and Washburn was presenting the idea to 31 school districts in northeast Kansas. That summer President Sponberg and Gerald K. Barker, who would lead the station in its formative years, made more than 50 appearances before various school boards and teacher groups.

By April 1965, Sponberg and Barker had signed up more than 80 schools and the machinery was put in place.

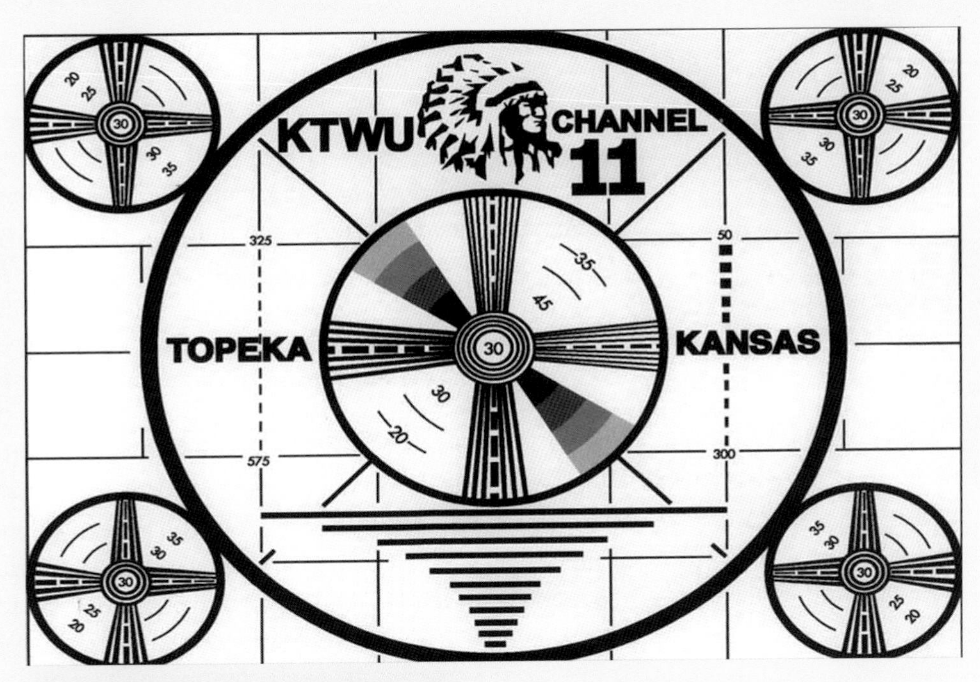

KTWU used a nationally standardized test pattern, which included a Native American in headdress, to help viewers adjust screens, above. Left: on the air.

The Garvey Foundation raised its commitment to $150,000. WIBW television of Topeka gave its old transmitting equipment and a lease on its transmitter building, and Washburn happily accepted.

Also, the federal Department of Health, Education and Welfare kicked in about $200,000.

Using channel 11, KTWU — its call letters standing for Topeka Washburn University — went on the air October 21, 1965.

Participation by school districts fell short of expectations and so did revenue, and after three months on the air Washburn contemplated ending the project. A $25,000 gift from Stauffer Publications rescued KTWU and station management went to work raising more money.

Its efforts worked and KTWU survived. In years to come, "educational television" would be re-branded "public television."

Georgia Neese Gray with Harry Truman and fellow honoree Robert Sarnoff.

Washburn would need to expand its graduate programs, continue to provide a high-quality undergraduate education, improve the library, and increase faculty and staff.

Somehow, they found, faculty morale remained high but understaffing was a problem, along with an inadequate library. Most problems could be traced to revenues that had not matched growth in spending. The accreditors' solution? More money from the state of Kansas.

State aid still was based on credit hours taken by undergraduates, meaning the Law School and graduate programs got no state money. In 1966, attempting to balance expenses with revenue, the Law School announced plans to limit its enrollment to 260, although it wound up allowing a few more in the fall semester.

As Henderson completed his first academic year as head of Washburn, the regents approved a tuition increase to help improve faculty salaries.

"We do not plan to expand numerically for the sake of 'getting larger,'" Henderson said at commencement time, repeating a thought from his inaugural. Instead, he preferred for Washburn to remain a general-interest university of "increasing quality."

At the June 1966 commencement, the university presented an honorary degree to Georgia Neese Gray, a Washburn alumna who was named the first female treasurer of the United States by President Harry S. Truman. For the occasion Truman and his wife, Bess, came to Topeka from their home in Independence, Missouri. Also honored was Robert W. Sarnoff, the president of RCA, the Radio Corporation of America and the NBC broadcasting network.

Hundreds of relatives and friends watched as 500 graduates received degrees at the city auditorium on June 5, a Sunday afternoon. Then the celebrities and the graduates departed. President John Henderson headed for a vacation in Wisconsin.

Washburn was about to begin what everyone expected to be a typical, quiet summer.

Washburn's picturesque campus, shaded aplenty in the 1960s by scores upon scores of mature trees.

Down, but Not Out

On the evening of June 8, 1966, Washburn had the undisturbed look that arrives when school is out. Trees planted decades before, some with boughs hanging barely above the grass, lined empty sidewalks. In the heart of campus, mid-20th-century buildings such as Morgan and Stoffer stood out against picturesque older buildings — Rice and Crane and MacVicar Chapel. This night, only a smattering of people were using any of them.

On the second floor of Carnegie, 40 law students reviewed for an upcoming bar exam. In another second-floor room, the American Institute of Banking gave tests in banking and data processing. At Benton Hall, 33 out-of-town girls settled in for a baton-twirling camp. At married students' housing, a few couples made dinner. And at MacVicar, faculty member Robert Snyder arranged seating for a music recital that would show off the talents of the 13 teenagers to whom he gave private music lessons. The recital would begin at 7 p.m.

Only three days earlier, the university had buzzed with commencement activity. Originally, ceremonies had been scheduled for this date, a Wednesday, but in February the event was moved to the weekend in hopes of attracting more visitors.

In its morning edition of June 8, *The Topeka Daily Capital* headlined "Tornadoes Dance in Sky Over Kansas," and told of twisters that had been spotted in other parts of the state the day before. Early June often shows a stormy side in Kansas, a fact of

Numbers
1980

» Topeka population: 118,690

» Washburn enrollment: 6,031

Path of the tornado across campus, looking southwest.

At WIBW, Bill Kurtis warned viewers in no uncertain terms: "For God's sake, take cover."

The tornado crossed Burnett's Mound, top, and headed for campus, eventually battering Rice Hall, above.

life to which Topekans were accustomed. For June 8, the prediction was rain.

Just as Snyder made the recital room ready, and as the rest of the hundred or so people on campus went about their tests and reviews and other chores, two strong storm cells developed southwest of Topeka. Soon afterward, they merged with a squall line.

At 6:50 p.m., the Weather Bureau issued a bulletin warning of heavy thunderstorms on the city's western edge. In that era, before cellular communications and the internet, bulletins clattered over teletype machines in law-enforcement offices and radio and television stations. At WIBW television, Washburn law student and part-time announcer Bill Kurtis went on the air to read the bulletins. Meanwhile, Topeka police stationed a patrolman at Burnett's Mound, a hill southwest of the city, to watch for any developments in the storm.

At Robert Snyder's music recital in MacVicar, about 40 parents and guests filed into the auditorium and took their seats. The recital began on schedule at 7 p.m.

About that moment, the Topeka policeman at Burnett's Mound picked up his radio microphone and called headquarters. He had spotted a tornado. A Kansas highway patrolman nearby reported it, too.

At 7:04 p.m., sirens sounded.

Hearing them, Snyder instructed his musicians and their audience to leave their seats and move downstairs to the safety of MacVicar's basement. It contained practice rooms with pianos so the instrumentalists would still have accompaniment. In the 1960s, the prevailing wisdom was to move to the southwest corner of a building, in the basement, if a tornado threatened. The piano in that corner, however, was out of tune, so Snyder looked for another spot and finally decided on his own studio in the southeast corner. Seating was arranged, everyone settled down and the recital began anew. Then the rain started.

At Carnegie, a librarian went to the room where the banking tests were under way. Over objections from the instructor, he persuaded the test-takers to head for the basement.

Top: The ruins of MacVicar Chapel, where a recital audience found safety in the basement. Stoffer Science Hall lost windows and walls, above left and right. At Boswell Hall, left, walls and roof suffered considerable damage.
Following pages: Amid a devastated campus, Crane Hall briefly withstood the storm and then collapsed as survivors looked on.

Workers wrapped Carnegie, which was chosen for restoration, to reduce further damage.

At 7:15 p.m. the tornado that only a few minutes before had been spotted by the policeman and the highway patrolman roared over Burnett's Mound. The police car was blown over, but the policeman survived.

The tornado coursed across southwest Topeka, heading northeast on a line that ran right at the Washburn campus.

At WIBW, Kurtis warned viewers in no uncertain terms: "For God's sake, take cover."

In the basement of MacVicar, there was no TV. As the second recitalist played his bassoon solo, the rain grew noisy. MacVicar's basement was actually a half-basement, and it had windows. As the recital audience glanced up, the windows were spattered by driving mud. The wind roared. Lights flickered off. Everyone in the room crawled under chairs, piano benches — anything. Worried about his bassoon, the young musician lay on top of it.

The tornado entered the northern half of campus, the built-up part, the part where it would do the most damage. It ripped past sorority houses and over a parking lot. Its winds tore at Benton Hall and demolished the Air Force ROTC building.

The tornado plowed past Crane Observatory, and over Thomas Gymnasium and Boswell Hall. It slammed into Carnegie and MacVicar, and blew past Rice.

Then, the twister passed Stoffer, where an electric clock inside stopped at 7:21 p.m.

From there, the storm ripped on to the Central Park neighborhood northeast of campus and then to downtown Topeka, where it brushed the Capitol, knocked down houses, badly damaged businesses and overturned cars before lifting to the northeast. That ended its path across the city — and through the heart of Washburn.

When the noise outside stopped, Robert Snyder, his music students and their audience in the basement of MacVicar looked around them. The 76-year-old building had collapsed on itself. Of the 40 people in the basement — teenage musicians, parents and guests — two people were cut by glass and there were a few bruises, but everyone survived. Some felt severe pain in their ears, probably from the change in air pressure as the twister blasted through the campus. Most of the basement was filled with wreckage, much of it fallen from what had been the upper stories of MacVicar.

By 1967, buildings were repaired. Washburn's once-plentiful campus trees would take years to recover.

Climbing out of the debris, the recital-goers stared at ruined buildings and fallen trees. The roaring wind had denuded the few trees still standing and ripped up lawns.

Lloyd Durow

Richard Vogel

Other people emerged from other campus buildings. Crane Observatory was standing when they came out. As they watched, it began to collapse.

A banking student who had been taking the test in Carnegie — his test papers now blown away — rushed outside to look for his 1966 Volkswagen. He found it, resting in what was left of a tree. At Stoffer, wind-driven sand pitted the lens of the seven-decades-old telescope. Its dome was ripped away.

All told, the tornado had taken 26 minutes to travel 12 miles on the ground across the city and scraped a path a half-mile wide. Seventeen people died in it, 14 of them inside the Topeka city limits, and more than 400 were injured. No one died on the Washburn campus.

About a half-hour after the tornado passed, Lloyd Durow, head of physical operations for Washburn, drove to the campus with his wife alongside him in their car. Police blocked the street approaches, so Durow left the car to walk the final few hundred yards. He told his wife to return home and not to expect him for a long time.

After surveying the damage for hours,

Durow went to the home of Richard Vogel, Washburn's financial vice president, who had begun poring over insurance appraisals and statements of value through what would be a sleepless night. With President Henderson in Wisconsin, Vogel was running things along with the vice president for academic affairs, Arthur Engelbert.

At one point, a newspaper reporter caught up with Durow and asked him about the future.

"There'll always be a Washburn," Durow replied.

Aiming to make much the same point, Engelbert conferred with the chairman of the Washburn Board of Regents and proceeded to WIBW. The station broadcast his assurances to faculty, students and the city that Washburn would survive.

Arthur Engelbert

For Washburn, almost everything physical had changed. Classrooms, offices, laboratories, practice rooms and meeting halls that for decades had served students, faculty and staff were gone. The campus was a mess. Debris would have to be removed, insurance companies contacted and temporary buildings provided. Then would come the biggest problem: Deciding what to rebuild and when.

Yet if physical things changed, much else remained the same. As had happened so many times in its past, Washburn faced calamity with resolve and stared it down.

Recovering

The day after the tornado, cranes and wrecking crews went to work. Two days later, Washburn began summer classes. The regular work of the university stayed on schedule — but not on campus. Washburn rented classroom space from Topeka West High School. At Morgan Hall, administration offices reopened within five days. In temporary quarters, the university continued to function.

Help came in the form of hundreds of gestures, large and small. Hours after the

90 and a survivor

The morning after the tornado struck, Gerald K. Barker, assistant to the president, made his way to the mission-style home built on campus by former President Parley Womer and his wife. Womer had died in 1957, but Verna Womer still lived there. She was 90 years old and Barker worried that she might have left the house or been injured.

Barker knocked on the door. Verna Womer answered, assuring him she was all right despite considerable damage to the home.

What had she done to survive the tornado? Barker asked.

"I just stayed in the living room," she replied. "I thought if the good Lord wanted to take me in a Kansas tornado, He could have me."

tornado, the property superintendent from the University of Kansas arrived with a 12-man crew and a generator. His staff electricians, working through the night, restored Washburn's power.

Volunteers started to clean things up. The effort gained a name: Operation Ichabod. Crews placed tarpaulins and plastic sheeting atop the ruined structures. What remained of the law library was moved to the basement of the city library and later to a warehouse near Forbes Air Force Base. Law firms and law-book publishers replaced many of the lost volumes.

On June 10, President Lyndon Johnson declared Shawnee County a disaster area and the next day Corps of Engineers equipment arrived to begin clearing debris.

Only six months earlier, Washburn had increased its insurance coverage to replacement cost from depreciated value. That was fortunate timing, because it was soon determined that nearly two-thirds of the buildings that had stood on campus were damaged or destroyed.

Rice Hall — opened in 1874 and now 92 years old — was declared a total loss. The same went for Boswell Hall, built in the 1880s, and MacVicar Chapel, Crane Observatory, Thomas Gymnasium and the Air Force ROTC structure.

New buildings would cost far more than their predecessors. The rebuilding effort would be staggering. Insurance adjustors spent two months on campus, meeting with administration representatives nearly every day. The insurors and the university finally settled on a $2.879 million loss — equal to roughly $20 million in 21st-century dollars.

By the end of June contracts were signed for demolition and removal of debris, and for repairs to Morgan and Stoffer, neither even a dozen years old, along with Whiting, Benton and Carruth. Demolition crews finished their work by August 31, before the fall semester began. Through July and August, wreckers hauled away more than 500,000 tons of debris.

Insurance would have covered demolition and reconstruction of all the older buildings, but alumni pleaded with the administration to save at least one. Five months earlier, on Founders Day, Henderson had pledged to renovate Rice Hall, which dated to 1874. But the tornado had taken too much of it. Among the older structures, Carnegie, built as

"There'll always be a Washburn."

— Lloyd Durow, physical operations manager, in the hours after the tornado.

Reinstalling the telescope mount in Stoffer Science Hall.

1966-1997

The phoenix, a metal statue presented to the university in 1967 as a symbol of rebirth after the tornado. It is displayed in the lobby of White Concert Hall.

1966: On June 8, a tornado roared through Washburn, causing millions of dollars in damage. Summer school and the fall semester continued as normal.
— Amid the rebuilding, an addition to Memorial Union opened.
1967: A time capsule including, among other things, a tornado insurance claim report, was placed in the cornerstone of a three-story addition to Morgan Hall.
1968: October 29. The fine arts building was dedicated. A water feature, "Fountain of Learning," donated by the women's and men's honor societies, Nonoso and Sagamore, was activated.
1969: On September 27, the new Law School building was dedicated. Law classes had been in Carnegie before the tornado, and in metal trailers for three years afterward. The main speaker was Associate Justice Byron White of the U.S. Supreme Court.
— Women's intercollegiate basketball was restored after more than 60 years, and a women's volleyball team organized.
— Benton Hall became an all-male residence hall. Carruth was renovated to become all-female.
— In April, Verna Womer, widow of ex-President Parley Womer, died. The couple's home on campus was turned over to the university, which converted it to International House.
1971: University Place, housing for married students built in 1946, was removed.
— The Kuehne bell tower, containing the bells from Thomas Gymnasium, was built.
1973: The Department of Economics and Business Administration became the School of Business.
1974: Department of Nursing established.
1975: Fine arts building named the Garvey Fine Arts Center.
— Student Council reorganized and renamed the Washburn Student Association.
1976: Associate degree implemented.

Trailer "villages" were named for the buildings they replaced. This was Boswell Village.

a library and since converted to house the Law School, showed the best chance of renovation, even though early insurance estimates said it was 80 percent damaged. It was chosen to survive. Some of the stones used to rebuild it came from the razed buildings.

In place of the wiped-out classrooms and offices came 41 portable units — "relocatables," or trailers — provided by the federal government under the president's disaster declaration. Twenty-eight of the trailers measured 20 by 40 feet, and 13 more measured 40 by 40. All were anchored to concrete slabs. The Law School occupied eight of them.

The "temporary" units dotted the campus — some stood for years — causing wags to coin nicknames for Washburn such as "Tornado Tech" and "Instant University."

Neither students, faculty nor administrators loved the portable units. They proved costly to maintain, leaked in heavy rain and had poor acoustics and loud air-conditioning units. They simply were absolutely necessary.

In addition to the temporary structures, Washburn also received from the federal government more than $1 million in matching funds. Fund drives over the next two years raised the necessary match.

Before the tornado, Topekans admired Washburn's park-like campus, and not only because of its historic stone buildings. A tree-planting program begun in the 1880s by President Peter McVicar had gradually paid off in a forest of elms and other deciduous trees. Conifers flourished in a grove south of the student union — mostly Austrian and Scotch pines. Yet only trees that stood on the south

1977: Law School and Law Clinic addition completed.
1978: Mabee Library opened.
1979: Ground broken for Kuehne Hall, a dormitory.
1980: College of Arts and Sciences added a master's degree in clinical psychology to its only other graduate-level degree, elementary education. It expanded the latter to include middle school and secondary school certification.
— Kuehne residence hall opened.
1981: John Green became Washburn president.
1982: Go 4th celebration marked Independence Day. Fireworks and other festivities on Washburn campus were open to the public.
— The Washburn marching band, discontinued in 1967, was revived.
1983: In November, pre-enrollment was offered for spring semester 1984, ending traditional long lines on enrollment day.
— The School of Applied and Continuing Education was established with degrees in 18 fields. Later, it would become the School of Applied Studies.
1984: Whiting Field House was retired as home of Washburn's intercollegiate basketball teams and Lee Arena became their new home.
— The School of Nursing moved from tornado-era trailers into the Petro Allied Health Center.
1985: West residence hall opened.
1986: Ground was broken for Bennett Computer Center, which would house Prime 9750, the main academic computer.
1987: The name of the university endowment group was changed to the Washburn Endowment Association, ending 120 years of use of the name Washburn College Trustees. Since 1941, the Trustees had existed to raise money.
— The Sunflower Music Festival, a June series of free classical concerts, began.
1988: John Duggan became president, but died within months. Robert Burns was named interim president.
1988: The first episode of "Sunflower Journeys" aired in January on KTWU.
— On November 11, the Vietnam Veterans Memorial was dedicated.
1990: Hugh Thompson named president.
1994: KTWU moved to its new, on-campus building.
1996: Bradbury Thompson Alumni Center opened.

part of the campus made it unscathed through the tornado; on the northern portion, 600 trees were destroyed.

The comeback

When fall semester 1966 began, students walked from class to class through a bleak landscape dotted by temporary trailers and marked by wide expanses of dirt. Fall enrollment barely exceeded 4,000, down from about 4,500 in fall 1965. Most of the decrease came in the freshman class; the previous year's freshmen, along with sophomores and juniors, had stayed the course. Indeed, confidence in Washburn's ability to survive showed itself amply among students, faculty, administrators and alumni.

Morgan west wing under construction, 1966-1967.

Engelbert had worried that faculty would leave because of the setback. To his relief, none did. Alumni and students came through with contributions. In October, a men's pep club called the WUlf Pack marked the north end of Moore Bowl with the letters "WU" in masonry. One year later, a metal statue of a phoenix, symbolizing rebirth, was presented to the university by the Arnold Air Society and Angel Flight, two organizations related to Air

Students laid out the college initials at Moore Bowl, 1966, top left. Top right: Punch cards, symbol of 1967 computer technology. Above: Dedication of the new Law School building in 1969.

Force ROTC.

Rebuilding continued through the 1966-1967 school year. In fall 1967 Carnegie reopened as the home for the Education Department.

An addition to the 14-year-old Memorial Union, under way before the tornado, was completed and opened in late 1966, more than doubling the space there.

And new buildings rose.

The Fine Arts Building, for which planning had begun before the disaster, opened in October 1968, joined to the Mulvane Art Museum. The museum itself stood through the tornado, but its roof and windows required considerable repair. In 1975, the complex would be renamed the Garvey Fine Arts Center, after its donors, Ray and Olive Garvey.

Morgan Hall received an addition with new classrooms in 1967, and the university mounted four clock faces on its tower. A new building for the Law School was finished in 1969, allowing law professors and students to move out of their trailer classrooms and offices.

A Learning Resources Center opened in 1971. In 1976, it would be named for President Henderson.

Washburn preserved remnants of its destroyed buildings. Four bells from the clock tower of Thomas Gymnasium were installed in 1971 in the new Kuehne Bell Tower, where they chimed the hour, half-hour and quarter-hours. Two concrete pillars from MacVicar Chapel were installed at the end of a parking

At work in a studio at the Mulvane Art Museum, above. Mabee Library, left.

lot and, after years in storage, a stained-glass window from Boswell was hung in the lobby of White Concert Hall.

Trees, too, were replaced. At Christmastime 1966, Washburn's Alumni Association urged supporters to purchase live holiday trees that could be planted on campus. Three Topeka nurseries agreed to pick them up after the holidays and plant them for free, and as a result the campus gained more than 200 new conifers. Scores of individuals and organizations donated trees, and soon the campus was dotted with new growth.

Five years after the tornado, classrooms

and other space lost in the storm had been replaced and even more buildings were on the drawing boards.

In 1973, the Mabee Foundation of Tulsa promised $500,000 to Washburn for a new library, provided that Washburn match that amount. In July 1974, the foundation agreed to give an extra quarter-million dollars, and students pitched in with fundraising efforts. In 1978 the Mabee Library opened.

On the horizon in the 1980s would be new residence halls, an allied health center and more.

Campus serenity

Unlike some other campuses in Kansas, Washburn mostly avoided the wave of student demonstrations in the late 1960s and early 1970s. In June 1969, President Henderson reported to the Board of Regents that the university "has been free of campus disorder and riots." The Washburn Air Force ROTC department had encountered no problems with anti-war protests.

Nevertheless, administrators met with Topeka police to plan responses to any upheavals. Henderson said in 1970 that extra security had been hired in "periods of tension" in the city and down the Kaw at the University of Kansas — where demonstrations had occurred frequently and where some campus buildings had been damaged and burned.

One of Washburn's few moments of public anti-war protest occurred in early May 1970, when a group of students lowered the U.S. and Kansas flags to half-staff in the wake of the shootings of students at Kent State University in Ohio. Someone else raised the flags back to the top, and then a compromise was reached in which only the Washburn flag

The entrance to White Concert Hall at the Garvey Fine Arts Center.

WUlf Pack student cheering section in Moore Bowl bleachers, late 1960s.

was flown at half-staff. Four pine trees were planted at 17th street and Washburn Avenue as a permanent memorial to the four people who died at Kent State.

There were, nevertheless, undercurrents of a different restlessness. By the mid-1970s, Henderson faced faculty and student tension over university governance, and specifically over how much authority the administration should share. In Henderson's annual report to the regents, he gave it a name: "the rampant growth of 'involvement'." He dismissed the movement as "a current fad."

Nationwide, professors and students sought a bigger role in the workings of higher education; Henderson fretted about this push for "participatory" democracy in administering the college. He worried aloud about segments of the Washburn community that wanted a hand in running things — even deciding on budgets — without the knowledge or experience to do it well. Those decisions, he assured the regents, should rest with them.

By 1976, Henderson proudly reported to the regents that harmony prevailed.

" 'Anti' efforts were usually throttled early in the embryo stages," he said. "Any attempts to stir up 'issues' and opposition to ongoing activities were totally thwarted."

A year later, Henderson saw "absolutely no anti-establishment feelings that prevailed from 1965 to 1973."

In 1974, a short-lived springtime fad called "streaking" — in which men and women ran naked through streets or disrupted events — struck Washburn, as it did many other campuses.

With streaking, nothing much political was involved.

Money and demographics

As it recovered from the tornado of 1966, Washburn found itself more than ever a public institution. In the 1970-1971 academic year, student tuition and fees composed about 43 percent of the budget, a substantial portion yet a far cry from the two-thirds that student money represented before the college became a municipal institution. Topeka taxpayers now provided about 23 percent of the university's revenues and state taxpayers 15 percent, which was the largest part of what was left.

Four years later, Henderson reported that state aid had outstripped tax support from the city. Indeed, the Topeka mill levy had remained the same since 1956.

Inflation had not stayed the same. At

Led by marchers carrying a banner and a flag-draped coffin, students walked from the Union to the flagpole as part of a memorial service in May 1970 for the four students shot to death at Kent State University in Ohio.

Left: President Henderson refused requests to lower U.S. and Washburn flags to half-staff; the next day the Student Council voted to lower the Washburn flag alone.

times in the 1970s running at 10 percent, the continuing increase in the price of things concerned administrators, who worried about paying for them and about the impact on student fees. Increases in student fees, naturally, posed a threat to enrollment.

As always, Topekans dominated the class rolls, which in fall 1970 numbered almost 4,800. In the 1970-1971 year, 46 of every 100 Washburn students were graduates of a Topeka high school. Thirty-five of 100 came from other places in Kansas.

Washburn students tended to be older than average. The typical age at graduation for a four-year student entering directly from high school was 22. At Washburn, 51 percent were older than 22. Military veterans represented an increasing proportion of students; by spring 1974 Washburn would count about 800. Among all students, one in three was married.

In years to come, Henderson was to remark that the student body remained "heavily involved in outside employment and tends to take less than a full load."

At the beginning of the 1970s, part-time students — presumably working full-time and taking courses in their spare hours — represented 30 percent of Washburn students. By 1980, the number would grow to 45 percent of the total. More than half would be 25 or older, compared with 35 percent of college students that age around the country. The average age of Washburn students would remain 26.

"Non-traditional" students were becoming the norm at Washburn.

Adapting to workplace demands for more career-oriented classes and degrees, Washburn in 1973 transformed the Department of Economics and Business Administration into the School of Business and in 1982 began offering a master's degrees in business administration.

Bowls, championships, women's intercollegiate teams return

For the first time in the history of Washburn football, the 1974 Ichabods played in a post-season game, the Boot Hill Bowl in Dodge City. Washburn beat Milliken University of Decatur, Illinois, 21-7.

The Ichabods had left the Central Intercollegiate Conference in 1968, spent three seasons in the Rocky Mountain Athletics Association and four more in the Great Plains Athletic Conference.

In 1976, Washburn moved to the Central States Intercollegiate Conference and returned to the Boot Hill Bowl the same year, losing to Benedictine.

In 1981, the men's and women's track teams, suffering from low participation, were disbanded, and the next year the sports program was upended with a new athletic director and a new football coach.

In 1983, the Ichabod footballers posted a record of eight victories and two losses and won the conference championship under Coach George Tardiff. In 1986, under Coach Larry Elliott, Washburn played to an 8-3 regular-season record, appeared in an NAIA postseason game and traveled to Mexico City for the Aztec Bowl, defeating a group of Mexican all-stars. The Ichabods joined the Mid-America Intercollegiate Athletics Association in 1989. They have been members ever since.

From 1966 to 1997, the men's basketball team — under only two coaches the entire time — won 10 conference championships and went only three years without a winning record. Coach Glenn Cafer oversaw the team through 1979, then Bob Chipman took over.

Women's basketball in 1981, above; the Boot Hill Bowl in Dodge City in 1976, below.

In March 1987, Washburn won the NAIA national championship, defeating West Virginia State at Kemper Arena in Kansas City, Missouri. The score was 79-77.

Women's sports saw a resurgence in the 1960s. Teams were organized in gymnastics, volleyball, field hockey and basketball. After Title IX in 1972 outlawed discrimination based on sex, the women's athletic budget was increased.

The women's intercollegiate basketball team, disbanded more than six decades before, was restored in 1969 under coach Jan Nuzman. The team won its first conference championship under coach Patty Dick in the 1983-1984 season, then three straight in the 1986-1989 seasons and one more in 1993. In 23 seasons, Dick's teams won 431 games.

The 1987 Ichabods stood for the team portrait, top, and celebrated after winning the NAIA championship, above. They received congratulations from Governor Mike Hayden, right.

The Henderson Learning Resources Center in the 1970s, right, and a lecture hall inside it, below.

The university established a bachelor's degree in nursing in 1974. Eight years later, the program would become the School of Nursing.

As Washburn created more courses outside the liberal arts, it established Special Instructional Programs in the 1970s. The division encompassed continuing education as well as a range of courses including child development, gerontology, mental health and drug counseling. In 1983, it was renamed the School of Applied and Continuing Education.

In 1970, Law School enrollment had soared to 600 students, a number that administrators thought approached saturation. The number of sociology students had more than doubled since the year before the tornado, and communications enrollment had risen 58 percent. On the other hand, enrollment in foreign-language classes dropped nearly 60 percent in five years. Astronomy and physics, American citizenship and education also lagged in enrollment.

By 1978, Henderson was describing Washburn as an "evolving urban university." New majors were devised to respond to the needs of students living in the modern city. Washburn added two-year degrees in criminal justice, child development, community health, computer science, aviation and other fields. In 1976, the university opened a Gerontology Institute, aimed at providing educational opportunities for older adults.

Many students had a job nearby and were enrolled because they wanted to improve their status at work or because they had already embarked on one career and now sought a new one. In 1979, one-fifth of all credit hours taken in the College of Arts and Sciences and in the Business School were in night classes.

A change in leaders

In spring 1980, friction grew between President Henderson and some members of the Washburn Board of Regents over various matters, including administrative salaries. For months, Henderson and his foes went back and forth.

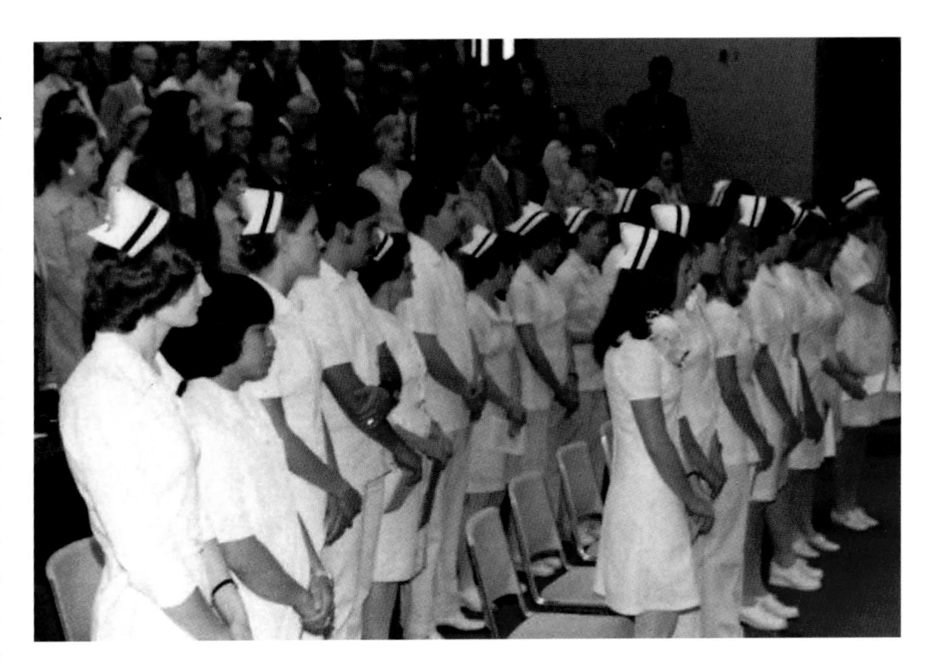

The first class to graduate from the nursing program, 1976.

Matters came to a head on December 10, 1980. At the end of a routine regents meeting, Henderson announced that he would step down at the end of spring semester 1981. Then he would become president of the Washburn College Board of Trustees, which since 1941 had served strictly as an organization that managed and worked to increase the endowment of the municipal university.

As Henderson prepared to leave office, the Kansas Legislature in late spring 1981 altered the makeup of the Washburn Board of Regents. To that point, the Topeka School District had four appointments to the board. The Legislature removed the school board's appointing power, giving four appointees to the Topeka City Council, three to the governor and one to the state Board of Regents. The mayor would remain the ninth Washburn regent.

Whatever the reason for Henderson's departure, he had presided over dramatic changes in Washburn. Rebuilding the university from ruins, creating a new infrastructure where once had stood buildings a half-centu-

Following pages: Washburn Room in the Memorial Union, 1980s.

In the late 1970s, electric typewriters still had uses, top. Electric keyboards served a mid-1980s music course, above.

ry or more old was a job he never envisioned when taking office. And there were equally large changes in what the school offered its students.

As one official put it several years later, in the 1960s Washburn basically had been a liberal arts college with a law school attached. In the ensuing years, it became a "multi-university" with far more choices for students. The transformation was well under way when John Henderson left office.

Also by 1980, Washburn was the only remaining municipally supported university in the United States.

A new president

Henderson was replaced quickly. By the end of June 1981, the Washburn regents chose for the presidency John L. Green Jr., most recently a top administrator at the University of Miami and before that the University of Houston system.

Green promptly restructured the administration and made academic deans responsible directly to him instead of to the vice president for academic affairs. He also found that Washburn had a low profile outside Topeka. And it was missing a full-time, energetic fundraising program and an annual giving campaign.

Early in his tenure, Green acknowledged that sentiment had been building in Topeka and among the regents to make Washburn a fully state-supported school under the Kansas Board of Regents, like the University of Kansas, Kansas State, Emporia State and others. The idea went back at least as far as 1960, when it had been broached in a study of higher education in Kansas. Surely, such a move would appease Topeka individuals and businesses who considered Washburn a tax burden and who knew their property tax rates typically ranked among the highest two or three in the state.

However, the new president resisted the idea, seeing "no apparent advantage" in the move. Delay it, he recommended, and study other revenue possibilities. He was able to persuade the Washburn regents to hold off.

Instead, Green proposed higher tuitions and in spring 1982, Washburn announced a 25 percent increase. He also created a separate staff to recruit new students. That fall, despite the tuition hike, enrollment increased by more than 6 percent. At the same time, state revenues declined. Washburn did the unheard-of, giving back 4 percent of the money the state had provided.

Meanwhile, the university embarked on a whirlwind of new programs and activities. Marking the dawn of the information age, Washburn in 1982 began offering new majors in computer science and information systems. Use of the university's Academic Computing Center increased from 730 users in fall 1982 to more than 2,000 in fall 1985. The Charles R. Bennett Computer Center was built to meet that need. The building, containing computer labs for students and the university's information technology department, opened in 1988.

The American Citizenship Program, begun in the 1920s by Parley Womer with an Eastern donor's money, was split into a department of history and a department of political science in 1983. Also added was a bachelor's degree in public administration.

Washburn opened an office of minority affairs and expanded the hours classes were offered to accommodate working students.

In 1983, the university organized a $23 million-plus capital campaign called "Making the Difference." By 1984 it had raised more than $18 million and reached the $23 million goal in 1985, a year and a half early. Nevertheless, the campaign continued, eventually reaching $38 million.

Meanwhile, the regents decided to proceed with the new Allied Health Center, which promised to become the largest building on campus. It would house the School of Nursing, health and physical education programs, intercollegiate athletics offices and a new basketball arena, finally replacing the 1928 arena in Whiting. Instead of razing Whiting Field House, the old building was incorporated into plans for the larger health center.

When the new building was dedicated in 1984, it bore the name Petro Allied Health Center after donors Kelsey and Edna Petro of

Computer lab in the 1980s.

Karl Menninger, co-founder of the Menninger Clinic and a world-renowned psychiatrist, enrolled in Washburn in 1910, left, and departed before graduating to study elsewhere. He came back in the early 1920s, taught psychology and criminology until 1960 and returned in 1982 to teach criminal justice.He died in 1990 at age 96.

John Green, president from 1981 to 1988.

Topeka. The new arena inside was named for another donor, Robert Lee of Topeka.

The 1985 graduating class numbered 960 — second largest in the history of the school. Enrollment topped 7,000 in 1984 and hovered around that number for years afterward.

Along the way, Green made big proposals for increasing the size and status of Washburn. Among them were to increase enrollment to 10,000 by 1990, to expand its tax support, to strengthen its image and to build more on-campus housing until 10 percent to 15 percent of students lived on campus. He also dreamed of upgrading Washburn's athletic programs and of joining the Missouri Valley Conference.

Through his tenure, critics pointed out, tuition more than doubled. Part of that was because his administration coincided with a high-inflation period in U.S. history. Green responded to the criticism in 1987 by cutting his own salary 3.8 percent.

In 1983, the university organized a $23 million-plus capital campaign called "Making the Difference." By 1984 it had raised more than $18 million and reached the $23 million goal in 1985.

In his self-evaluation, Green's most important accomplishment was the accreditation of all Washburn programs by the North Central Association. He was also proud of his night-school Masters in Business Administration, part of a wave of such programs across the country, which allowed students to continue their regular work while earning an MBA.

"Statehood"

Despite Green's successful efforts to raise money and his early aversion to joining the state regents system, the matter did not die. In April 1985, the Washburn regents voted to ask the Legislature to consider state affiliation and by September the regents were referring to its "inevitability." By early 1986 even Green was calling the move inevitable. In May 1986, Green told the regents that he intended to step down when his contract expired in June 1988. Meanwhile, he promised to work to carry out the regents' wish and move toward becoming part of the state system. If the move succeeded, he said, the state Board of Regents would then have the chance to name its own president.

The state affiliation effort — "statehood" for short — continued in 1987 but, amid constraints on state revenue, the matter was put off again. The Legislature did find enough money to send Washburn $200,000 — the first state funds not tied to credit-hour enrollment.

In 1989, when state affiliation came back before the Legislature, proponents found opposition stronger than anticipated. Detractors, among them civic leaders and newspaper editors from towns that held existing state institutions, argued that adding Washburn would only further divide the revenue pie. Each school, the opponents feared, would get less if Washburn entered the group. Also, some argued there were too many state schools near Topeka already.

Even some Washburn backers complained that the university might lose its identity by joining the state system. Others feared that the Law School would be closed, merged with KU's or moved to Wichita.

Turned back again, proponents of state affiliation looked around to see what money Washburn could get. The Legislature responded, providing the biggest increase in state aid in 10 years. Now state aid totaled $1.2 million and represented 26 percent of the university's annual budget.

Also approved by legislators was an

From the Ichabod's originator, a new kind of Bible

Bradbury Thompson, designer extraordinaire.

Bradbury Thompson, born in Topeka and a member of Washburn's graduating class of 1934, brought the *Kaw* yearbook to new heights of design in the 1930s, first as a student and continuing as a consultant after graduation. In 1938, he introduced the first visual representation of the Ichabod as a symbol of the school.

Then Thompson embarked on a career that took him to the East Coast and to the top of the world of graphic design. He became design director of *Art News,* art director of *Mademoiselle*, created the format for Smithsonian magazine and turned out stamps for the U.S. Postal Service. Also, he taught generations of students at Yale University.

When Field Enterprises, a publisher of newspapers and encyclopedias, envisioned an elegant new collector's edition of the King James version of the Bible, it turned to Bradbury Thompson to design it. The project would be published in large format with fine art accompanying the scripture. In 1969, Thompson set to work. He chose a handsome font for the text and arranged every verse and phrase with breaks where a reader might naturally pause. He worked with the director of the National Gallery of Art to select appropriate classical paintings of Biblical scenes.

Then came the recession of the early 1970s, and Field Enterprises gave up the idea.

Lest his work go for naught, Thompson in 1977 approached Washburn alumna Olive White Garvey, matriarch of a family that had contributed large amounts of money to Washburn.

Thompson suggested that his Bible be printed under the imprimatur of the Washburn College Board of Trustees — an expensive proposition for the ultra-high-quality volume. Proceeds from sales would support the university, a task befitting the trustees as the university's fundraising arm. Thompson's persuasiveness was effective, Garvey agreed and her daughter, Ruth Garvey Fink, was named to head a committee to oversee the project.

In 1979 a three-volume limited edition with 10-inch-by-14-inch pages entitled *The Washburn College Bible* was published, selling for $2,500 a set. Three hundred ninety-eight sets were produced and by mid-1981 sales had netted more than $300,000. A smaller, one-volume version was printed the next year by the Oxford University Press and it gained wide distribution through the Book-of-the-Month Club.

Thompson's Bible would be called the most monumental makeover of the Bible's typography since Gutenberg's edition of 1455. It was regarded as his masterpiece.

Thompson, died in 1995 at 84. His name is memorialized in the Washburn alumni center, built in part with revenue from sales of the book. The center's architect was Thompson's son, Mark Thompson, an architect based in Philadelphia.

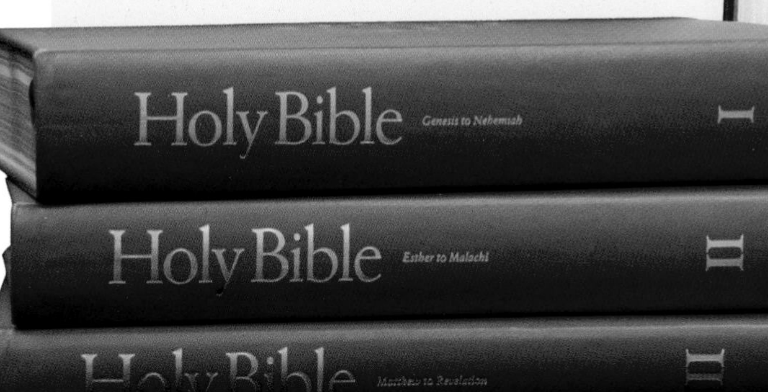

The language lab.

A family of benefactors

The names on the Garvey Fine Arts Center and White Concert Hall hint at the impact on Washburn of multiple generations of a Kansas family. Other familiar Washburn projects — KTWU and the *Washburn College Bible* — also owe much to the Garveys.

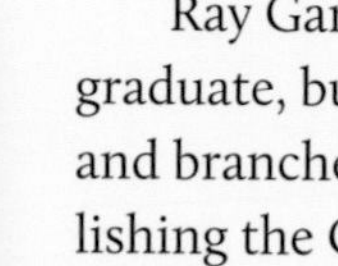

Olive White Garvey

Ray Garvey, a 1914 Washburn law graduate, built his fortune in Kansas wheat and branched out to other projects, establishing the Garvey Foundation as his philanthropy. After he died in 1959, his widow, Olive White Garvey, also a 1914 graduate, made possible foundation support for the fine arts center and for the concert hall, which was named after her brother, Elliot White, also a Washburn alumnus.

Their daughter, Ruth Garvey Cochener Fink, continued the family tradition, supporting the *Washburn College Bible* and the Bradbury Thompson Alumni Center. Her son, Bruce Garvey Cochener, was a trustee of the Washburn Foundation and established multiple Washburn scholarships.

Garvey Fine Arts Center, which includes White Concert Hall

increase in the university's portion of Topeka property taxes from 2.25 mills to 3 mills. That allowed Washburn to issue bonds to complete an addition to the Law School and to upgrade KTWU's facilities.

As promised, Green stepped down as president at the end of the school year in 1988 and became a member of the faculty at the Washburn Business School. From there, he went on to head business-school accrediting associations and a senior-citizen advocacy group, all based in the Kansas City area.

An untimely end

To succeed Green, the regents chose John M. Duggan. He held degrees from the College of the Holy Cross and from Yale, had taught and been an administrator at Vassar, and most recently had worked for the Foundation for Independent Higher Education, a national association for state and regional independent college fund-raising associations.

Duggan, 60, was viewed as energetic and able, and on July 1, 1988, he began his job with vigor. Among his top priorities was a renewed push for state affiliation for Washburn. He traveled to the campuses of the other Kansas colleges and universities, meeting with their chief executive officers. He also journeyed across Kansas, meeting with alumni and friends of Washburn — and with civic leaders and newspaper editors who opposed Washburn's state affiliation.

"No other university in the country," Duggan wrote in the *Alumni Review*, "continues to receive the amount of local tax support which Washburn enjoys." He did not believe Topekans could bear the burden much longer, nor could its students continue to pay what was the highest tuition of any public university in the region.

Duggan's ceremonial inauguration took place October 16, 1988, at Lee Arena. Two weeks later, as he continued to travel through Kansas, he became ill and was hospitalized. On November 25, his illness was diagnosed as pancreatic cancer, a rapidly spreading and deadly form of the disease. Five days later, on November 30, he died. Duggan, who was survived by his wife and five sons, was buried in Connecticut.

On December 6, less than two months after he was inaugurated, Duggan's memorial service took place at White Concert Hall.

According to many accounts, faculty, students and staff had taken well to Duggan. They liked his approach and admired his energy. His death after only a few months in office came as a tremendous shock.

When Duggan first fell ill, the regents chose Robert L. Burns, the vice president for academic affairs, as acting president. After Duggan's death, the regents changed Burns' title to interim president and put him in charge pending the selection of a permanent leader.

Burns, only recently promoted to vice president in Duggan's brief tenure, had come to Washburn two years before as dean of the College of Arts and Sciences. New as he was, he worked hard to strengthen ties with the faculty. He pushed for improvement in faculty salaries and testified often before legislative committees in favor of state affiliation.

He put forward his name for the presidency, becoming a finalist. But he would not get the job.

When a Washburn football player died with steroids in his possession, Burns ordered an investigation and the university began random drug testing of athletes, along with drug-education programs. He also did not renew the contract of the athletic director, but did not move to fire any coaches. His stand in the steroid matter, according to an editorial in *The Topeka Capital-Journal,* may have led to opposition to his being promoted to the presidency.

John M. Duggan

Robert L. Burns

Hugh L. Thompson

For the university's 125th anniversary in 1990, Bradbury Thompson designed a special Ichabod, updating his 1938 original with a pennant and a bird from the Washburn family crest.

Whatever the reason for Burns' being passed over, in February 1990 the regents chose Hugh L. Thompson, chancellor of the University of Indiana at Kokomo, to become Washburn president.

Shortly after Thompson's hiring was announced, accusations flew that the regents had violated the Kansas open meetings law by making the choice and offering a contract in private, only later taking a ceremonial public vote. The stir was large enough to call in the Kansas attorney general, Robert Stephan. Stephan found that Thompson's hiring had not violated Kansas law, but that the matter was "a close call."

The 'new majority'

Thompson officially took over August 1, 1990. As the century's last decade began, Thompson presided over a university with an enrollment of more than 6,300. The College of Arts and Sciences represented 65 percent of credit-hour enrollments. The rest were spread among the schools of Nursing, Applied and Continuing Education, Business and Law. Social work and criminal justice joined a reorganized School of Applied Studies and Continuing Education was split off it.

Since the tornado raked the campus 25 years before, Washburn had undergone a fundamental change in nature and outlook.

Rebuilding of Washburn's infrastructure was one thing. Its demographics were another. The "evolving urban university," as it was described in the late 1970s, continued to evolve into the 1990s. More and more students were older, held regular jobs, often took classes part-time and chose courses outside the traditional liberal arts.

In his fourth year as president, Thompson characterized the university as having two student bodies. One, comprising full-time students of traditional college age 18 to 24 years old, represented 45 percent of enrollment. The other — and now larger — portion was non-traditional, part-time students, averaging 28 years of age and carrying fewer than 12 credit hours.

"The new majority of students," Thompson said, "is the working adult with a family who enrolls intermittently on a part-time basis," many pursuing credit hours but not earning degrees.

Across America, he said, the fates of metro areas and the urban universities they contained were intertwined. Washburn was no different. The university had to be "integrated fully into Topeka and Shawnee County."

A survey of 350 graduates in 1995 showed that the school's location — not its faculty, nor its small class size, nor its athletic teams — was their No. 1 reason for attending Washburn. For many students, Washburn was simply "a means to an end," Thompson told an interviewer in 1996. School loyalty and affection for alma mater were weakened as a result.

"We don't have the kinship or affection or bonding, if you will, that can occur at other institutions," he said.

Only a few hundred students lived on campus; the rest attended classes but did not linger on campus for other activities. One faculty member recalled the campus looking deserted by 1 p.m. on weekdays, only to come to life again after 5:30 p.m. when part-time students got off work and arrived for class.

A world of competition

Efforts to join the state system kept going — and kept failing.

Thompson called affiliation part of an evolutionary process. Washburn students, he told a Kiwanis club meeting in 1991, still paid the highest tuition of any publicly supported university in the seven-state area, $82 per credit hour. At Kansas regents schools, he said, a credit hour cost students $45. An influx

A bonfire for homecoming, early 1990s.

of state money would change that imbalance.

Yet the idea still did not catch on. After the 1994 session of the Legislature once again refused to advance a bill that would have brought Washburn under the state Board of Regents, university lobbyist David Monical complained strongly.

"There are people who want and deserve a higher education who won't be able to receive one because of the chamber's action," Monical said. "It's the responsibility of the state, not the city, to provide higher education."

Opponents continued to argue that the Legislature had problems funding the six universities already in the system.

"It really doesn't make sense...to make the line longer and add one," said one senator from Overland Park.

Washburn was stuck with the formula for funding that had been in place since 1961: tuition plus income from its endowment plus state aid plus Topeka property taxes.

In 1995, Thompson told the faculty that the landscape for affiliation was turning bleak.

"We find ourselves in a competitive time and a hostile environment," he said. "Enrollment has declined slightly for several years and this trend cannot continue." Even on Washburn's home turf, Topeka, colleges both public and private were making inroads.

In late March 1996, after five years in the presidency, Thompson announced that he planned to retire with the end of his contract in June 1997. In the official announcement, Thompson noted that in May 1998 the university would undergo a reaccreditation. Making his retirement announcement early, he said, would allow time for the regents and his successor to prepare for that.

Thompson made the move seven hours after the Board of Regents held an executive session announced as being about a personnel matter. He had been excluded from that meeting and from similar meetings, hinting that his contract would not have been renewed. He was only days away from his 62nd birthday.

The Capital-Journal reported that some "of the school's faithful" held Thompson responsible for the failure to win state affiliation. On

The Bradbury Thompson Alumni Center, which opened in 1996.

stepping down, Thompson told a newspaper interviewer that he was disappointed about his ineffectiveness in the matter, particularly with voters and civic leaders in western Kansas and rank-and-file legislators. He called the school's lobbying effort "herky-jerky," the result of indecisiveness on how vigorously to make the push for affiliation.

"We haven't convinced the Legislature or the public," he said, "that Washburn is a state resource."

Eventually, Thompson would acknowledge that he had faced a range of difficulties on becoming president of Washburn, of which the controversy over the secret vote to hire him was only the first. Robert Burns, the interim who preceded Thompson, had been popular among the faculty, and had won the allegiance of many on campus. Also, upon entering office Thompson had been the fourth person in as many years to lead Washburn.

"I had to come in here and prove myself," Thompson would say later.

However, as his days wound down in June 1997, the *Capital-Journal* could point to successes as part of Thompson's legacy.

Besides new degree and certificate programs, they included the opening of the Bradbury Thompson Center in April 1996. The center, named after the man who drew the first Ichabod symbol in the 1930s and who designed the Washburn Bible, housed the Alumni and Endowment associations. Also the university's public television station, KTWU, moved to a new on-campus studio in 1994. State aid reached an all-time high.

The Washburn endowment reached $64 million in 1996, more than double its total at the end of 1989, and an addition to the Law School was built in 1992.

As for state affiliation, it was nowhere near. But another idea would take its place.

And coming to the fore was a matter touched on by Thompson as he left office: a push to add more "traditional" students to the "urban university."

Facing page: After Thomas Gymnasium was destroyed by the 1966 tornado, four bells that hung in its tower were saved and placed in the Kuehne Bell Tower, constructed in 1971. The bells ring the "Westminster Chimes" melody on the hour and at intervals between.

NCAA
NCAA
2005
DIVISION II
WOMEN'S
BASKETBALL
CHAMPIONSHIP
NATIONAL
CHAMPION

150 and Going Strong

Washburn rocketed into the 21st Century. The university rolled out its biggest building program since the years after the 1966 tornado and began remolding its student body. The Ichabods posted winning records in football, season after season, the women's basketball team won a national championship, and for the first time in recorded history Washburn had a president who considered it a bad year if he hadn't run 2,000 miles for exercise.

Jerry B. Farley took office as the university's 14th president on July 1, 1997. Upon arriving in Topeka, he hit the ground running, meeting with clubs, civic organizations, the governor and legislators and visiting the campuses of other universities and colleges in Kansas. Everywhere Farley showed up he wore a bow tie, bringing attention to himself and thus to the school, and symbolizing new things that lay on Washburn's horizon. At his alma mater, the University of Oklahoma, Farley had served as vice president for community relations and economic development. In his career in higher education, he had gained considerable experience in finance, including directing investments for faculty retirement funds.

Numbers

Population, 2010

- Kansas: 2,853,116
- Shawnee County: 177,934
- Topeka: 127,473
- Washburn enrollment: 7,230

Shoring up finances formed an important part of the new approach at Washburn, and so did putting up new buildings, but they were joined inescapably with another initiative: re-thinking

Number One: The 2005 women's national championship team.

1997-2014

1997: Jerry Farley named president of Washburn.
1999: Local tax shifted to Shawnee County sales tax; Topeka city property tax reduced.
– John Henderson, president of Washburn from 1965 through 1981, died.
2001: First students moved in to the Living Learning Center.
2003: The football stadium was refurbished, becoming Yager Stadium at Moore Bowl, and the Bianchino Pavilion replaced the old press box.
2004: The Carole Chapel was moved from the former Menninger Foundation campus to Washburn.
– Student Recreation and Wellness Center, Washburn Village and waterfall and rock garden at northeast corner of campus were completed.
2005: Art building opened.
– Washburn women won the NCAA Division II basketball championship.
2006: School of Business earned accreditation from the Association to Advance Collegiate Schools of Business - International.
2009: Whiting Field House, refurbished throughout, reopened with a weight room, practice courts, locker rooms and offices for the athletics program and faculty offices and classrooms for the School of Nursing.
2014: Work began on Kansas Bureau of Investigation's Forensic Science Building on campus.
– Makeover of Morgan Hall into a welcome center got under way.

Jerry Farley took over as president in 1997.

the demographics of the campus.

A home away from home

For decades, Washburn had accepted and even endorsed the idea that it was destined to be a commuter school with an average age much higher than the 18- to 22-year-old range of "traditional" college students. Indeed, many Washburn students came from Topeka and its environs, held regular daytime jobs and took courses when they could on evenings and weekends.

By the late 1990s, "even traditional-age students lived off campus," Farley recalls. There was a reason: Few places existed for them to live *on* campus. Now, the idea would be to alter that balance and to increase the number of traditional students, in hopes of creating a more cohesive "community of learning."

First, there would have to be a place for young students to sleep and to study. Within a couple of years, plans were announced for a 400-bed residence hall with common social and recreation areas and dining services. It would be called the Living Learning Center, and would be placed in the heart of campus. The target was the 18-year-old who planned to go directly from high school to college, the "traditional" student.

When planning began in 1999, the number of 18-year-olds graduating from Kansas high schools was projected to rise through the first decade of the 2000s. If Washburn intended to grow, it had to tap that market.

Studies found, however, that many parents outside Topeka balked at sending their 18-year-olds directly from home into off-campus housing. Before the Living Learning Center, "it was very difficult for a student from western Kansas to come here," Denise Ottinger, vice president for student life, told *The Topeka Capital-Journal*. "Parents aren't apt to let their children live in an apartment when they just finished high school."

Ground for the project was broken in April 2000 and the Living Learning Center began accepting residents in fall semester 2001.

Planners had another aim: increasing a sense of community, "to make a place where people feel they belong," as Farley described it. Campus, he said, should be a place for exchanging ideas.

"Students should have the opportunity to discuss what is happening in the classroom and their experiences, ideas and opinions," Farley said after the center opened.

In the heart of campus, Washburn's Living Learning Center.

"If everyone leaves campus after classes, that doesn't always happen."

So the Living Learning Center rose in the middle of things on the busy and built-up northern section of Washburn's 160 acres. Residents were required to have roommates, an attempt to nudge them away from spending too much time alone with cellphones and computers. Meeting rooms and kitchenettes formed part of the plan, along with housing for at least one faculty member and his or her family. The new building was attached to the Memorial Union, which was renovated

In fall 2002, Washburn reported 6,118 students enrolled. Credit-hours increased to the largest number since 1994. That year, Farley said Washburn would cap enrollment at 7,000. Many more students, it was thought, and class sizes would become too large.

In fall 2003, total enrollment passed 7,000. Full-time students totaled almost 4,600 and enrollment of freshmen and new students jumped 15 percent from the year before. The next year, total enrollment reached 7,400, breaking the record set in 1984. There, around the 7,000 mark, it remained well into the

By 2007, full-time students composed fully two-thirds of total enrollment, up from 45 percent in 1994.

Revenues 1998-99

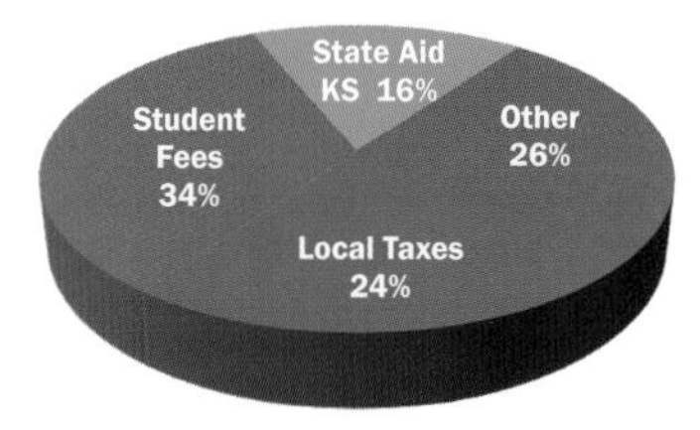

Revenues 1999-2000

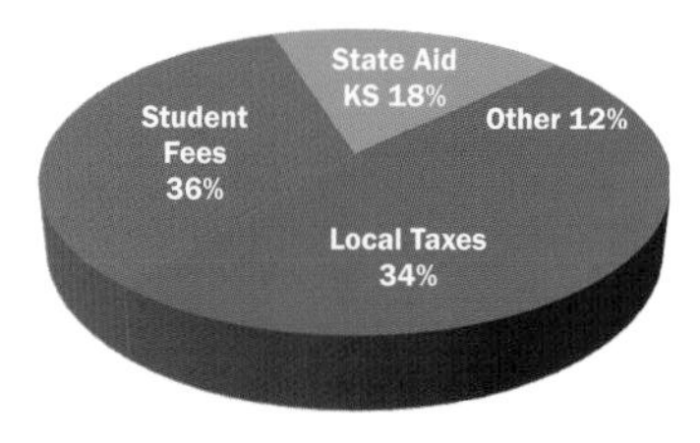

Addition of the Shawnee County sales tax, represented by the lower chart, altered the makeup of Washburn's income.

2010s.

By 2007, full-time students composed fully two-thirds of total enrollment, up from 45 percent in 1994. One in 10 lived on campus, and by 2010, the university had to create a waiting list for on-campus housing. In 2014, plans were announced for a new 350-bed, $30 million residence hall on the east side of the university grounds.

The revenue stream changes course

Within months after taking office, Farley was declaring that state affiliation no longer was "of paramount importance." He had decided, as he recalled years later, that the concept would never make it through the Legislature.

In fact, he says, state affiliation had never been the ultimate goal of the decades-long effort by Washburn leaders, only a means to another end: relieving the property taxpayers of Topeka. According to the Kansas League of Municipalities, Topeka property tax rates ranked for years among the highest in the state. By the 1980s, Topeka consistently stood first or second among the state's 20-odd largest cities. Washburn took a big chunk of that property-tax money.

Nevertheless, Washburn still needed public support. By March 1999, Topeka Mayor Joan Wagnon, the Shawnee County legislative delegation and Farley all supported a plan to shift the local burden from the property tax to a sales tax. The sales tax could be expanded beyond Topeka to include all of Shawnee County.

A sales tax, university officials pointed out, transferred as much as one-third of the tax burden to outsiders. Anyone who lived in neighboring counties — in fact, anyone traveling through the area from anywhere else — would help support Washburn simply by making a purchase from a Shawnee County retailer.

With prodding from Topekans, the Kansas Legislature in April 1999 enacted a law reducing the university's part of the Topeka property tax from 18.3 mills to 3.3 mills and allowing Washburn to levy a countywide sales tax of 0.65 of 1 percent.

The move to sales-tax revenue had the desired effect on Topeka property-tax rates, which have never again led the state. In most years since the change, Topeka has stood in eighth to 13th place among Kansas' larger cities and towns.

With that, Washburn's decades of trying and failing to gain "statehood" became a memory.

Even without state affiliation, Washburn had received state aid since the early 1960s. By the late 1990s, it had reached $5 million a year. Now, the university presented arguments to push that total higher.

In the fall 1997 freshman class, the first in Farley's presidency, 44 percent of students hailed from outside Shawnee County. Ninety-five percent were from Kansas. Despite the university's enrolling so many Kansans,

The art computer lab.

Holiday vespers performance at White Concert Hall. Vespers was first broadcast on KTWU in 2010.

however, state aid to Washburn averaged only $1,630 per student. Even community colleges received more from the state, $1,740 per student, and state Board of Regents institutions far more, $5,430. Should a school that serves so many Kansans, went Washburn's argument, not get more help from the entire state?

In 1999 the Legislature, encouraged by Farley and others, reorganized public higher education in Kansas. It moved community colleges from the state Board of Education to a reconstituted state Board of Regents and provided more money for many schools, among them Washburn. Although state aid now flowed through the state regents, governance of the university remained in the hands of Washburn's own Board of Regents. Washburn's annual request for state money was consolidated with all the other public colleges, universities and technical schools in Kansas, meaning Washburn's funding would rise and fall with the rest.

For Washburn, the result was positive. It promptly gained an extra $1 million a year. By the middle 2010s, Washburn was receiving $10 million a year from state taxpayers, about 12 percent of its operating budget.

On the field and court, more success

In 2003 Moore Bowl, nearly eight decades old, received a thorough renovation. An anonymous donor gave $1 million for the project and wanted the refurbished stadium named for Gary Yager, a former Washburn football running back who became a Topeka banker. The name was changed to Yager Stadium at Moore Bowl. The press box, a temporary structure put in place after the 1966 tornado, was replaced by a larger structure that included luxury suites. It was named the Bianchino Pavilion for Bernie Bianchino, a former Ichabod football player who got a degree from Washburn Law School, prospered in the telecommunications industry and donated $500,000 early in the campaign for athletic renovations.

The $4.3 million renovation of Moore Bowl presaged a string of football success longer than any other in Washburn history. In 2009, renovations were completed on Whiting Field House, the gymnasium built in 1928 as part of that era's expansion program. Until 1984, Whiting had housed Washburn basketball games, which were moved to the adjoining Petro Center. The remodeling, which left intact the stone exterior, brought a practice court, new weight rooms for student athletes, offices for the Sports Information Department and classrooms, labs and offices for the School of Nursing.

A national study found Washburn in the top 10 percent of public universities in return on its investment, and 30th among public schools in endowment per full-time-equivalent student.

The new weight rooms created with the renovation of Whiting contributed to success in other sports, too.

In 2005, the Washburn women won the NCAA Division II basketball championship. That came in the middle of a 51-game winning streak, the sixth longest in NCAA women's basketball history. They consistently made good showings in the NCAA post-season tournament under head coach Ron McHenry. McHenry, a Washburn alumnus, posted a 358-82 record in 14 seasons through 2014.

The men's basketball team made the playoffs again and again under longtime coach Bob Chipman, who had taken over the program in 1979. The Ichabods reached the national finals in 2001 and won multiple MIAA conference championships.

The football Ichabods, starting in 2004 under coach Craig Schurig, posted an unprecedented 10 winning seasons in the Mid-America Intercollegiate Athletics Association, a league of institutions from Kansas, Missouri, Oklahoma and Nebraska that Washburn joined in 1989. Washburn won the Mineral Water Bowl in 2004 and the Kanza Bowl in 2010, and reached the NCAA playoffs in 2005, 2007 and 2011. In the 2005 season, the Ichabods won the conference championship.

Change, the one constant

As the 21st century unfolded, the increasing numbers of potential freshmen that Washburn forecast in the late 1990s began to turn the other direction. By the early 2010s, there were fewer 18-year-olds in Kansas to tap. As a result, Washburn looked farther afield and offered lower in-state tuition to students from some western Missouri counties. Later, the lower tuition was expanded to students from all surrounding states plus Texas.

Projections showed the number of 18-year-olds from Kansas would begin to grow in the middle 2010s, but they would be increasingly culturally diverse, potentially requiring continued rethinking of the university's approach.

Meanwhile, Washburn opened some of its courses to students still in high school. Through the Concurrent Enrollment Partnership, certain courses at participating high schools are taught for college credit and with the same requirements as campus classes.

Facing page: The Bianchino Pavilion towered over players on the field of Yager Stadium at Moore Bowl at a 2011 game.

WASHBURN UNIVERSITY
BIANCHINO PAVILION

The Washburn Transformational Experience

On the theory that students experience life-changing moments outside the classroom as well as inside, Washburn in 2006 established the Washburn Transformational Experience. The program, at first required for graduation but later made voluntary, encourages students to pursue one or more of four "tracks." Students work under the supervision of faculty mentors. They must prepare written proposals before undertaking their projects and make reports or presentations after completion.

The community-service track calls for at least 150 hours of volunteer work in an acceptable non-profit organization and completion of a final project. Students have tutored preschool children, and worked in battered women's shelters and in nursing homes, among other places. The efforts are carried out under the umbrella of the Learning in the Community Program, or LinC, originally established as a student project in 1994. Aligned with LinC in the track is the Washburn Bonner Leader Program, which offers scholarships for community service through the Bonner Foundation of New Jersey. Bonner leaders also can qualify to earn money for service work.

The leadership track requires completion of a course and work in some leadership role. The track aims to help students assess their leadership skills and learn how to improve them. Independent study can be arranged through the Leadership Institute, which also offers a Leadership Studies minor and certificate.

Independent, individual projects are undertaken in the scholarly/creative track, which aims to help participants learn to sort through complex problems. Participants can create an original piece of music or art, write and produce a play, conduct an experiment, research a topic in depth or even start a business.

The international education track requires study abroad.

To help pay for the last two, Washburn makes available up to $1,000 a student.

The Transformational Experience began as a required program for graduation, and that requirement met with mixed reviews. Some students considered it burdensome and some faculty questioned whether the mandatory nature of the program hurt recruitment. Supporters pointed to surveys showing those who had completed the program had a positive experience and many students praised it.

The Transformational Experience became voluntary in 2010.

Amber Rufener, a LinC Bonner Leader, worked on a community garden in 2011.

Washburn Tech

In 2009, one year after management of the Kaw Area Technical School was shifted from the Topeka Board of Education to the Washburn Board of Regents, the regents changed the school name to the Washburn Institute of Technology.

The institute offers courses in construction, health care, computer and networking technology, business, transportation, hospitality and human services, and drafting and design. Through its classes, Washburn Tech provides a range of training for bookkeepers, legal and medical clerks, building tradespeople, cabinetmakers and millwork, HVAC technicians, electricians, industrial machinery troubleshooters, welders and other careers. It claims an 81 percent graduation rate, highest in Kansas among technical colleges. The institute serves 17 school districts.

Credits earned at Washburn Tech were made transferable to Washburn University.

Enrollment at Washburn Tech, about 640 in 2008, rose steadily, reaching 1,217 in 2014.

"It's one of the ways," President Jerry Farley said, "that we can prepare an educated workforce."

With the massive growth in internet access and ease of use beginning in the 1990s, Washburn also enrolled students who might never set foot on campus, in a classroom, dining hall, dormitory or recreation area. In colleges across America, the internet created the possibility of "distance learning."

Washburn formed alliances with community and technical colleges in Kansas and elsewhere to allow students with two-year junior-college associate degrees to complete a Washburn bachelor's degree and to do so online. Among the majors offered were health science, criminal justice and technology administration. Washburn called the program "2 + 2 Partnership for Learning and Networking" or "2+2 PLAN." An online student who lived far from Topeka would not have to leave home or quit a job to get a degree at Washburn.

A doctor of nursing practice progam, which prepares candidates for careers in management and leadership, exists predominantly online. Washburn also has created new master's programs in law, business, nursing and applied studies.

With the internet, "knowledge is ubiquitous," one longtime Washburn professor, Bill Wagnon, says. As a result, he believes, professors and colleges no longer are the main sources of knowledge, but still play key roles in helping people understand what's worth knowing.

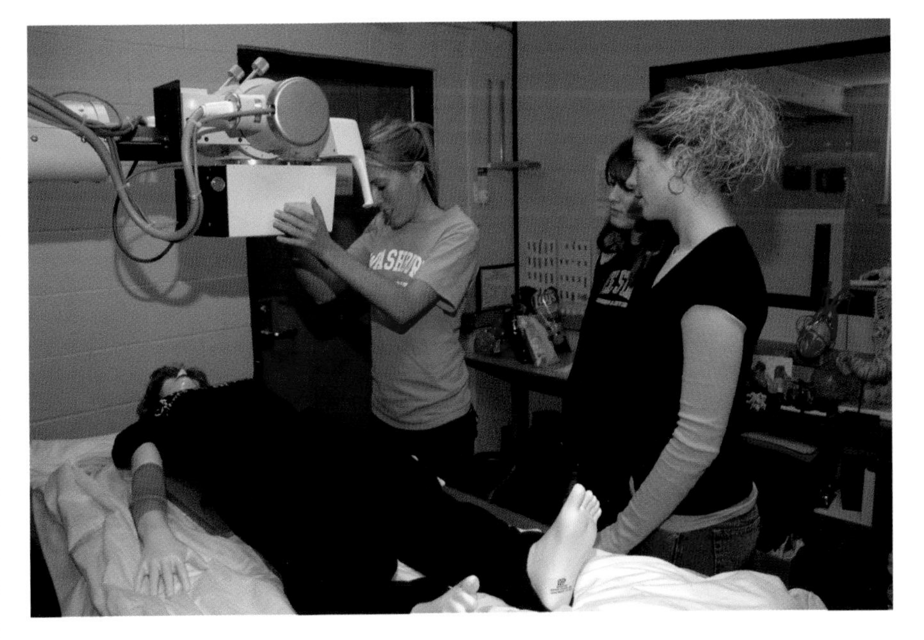

Students in the School of Applied Studies practiced techniques for imaging.

As late as the mid-2010s, it remained unclear how successful online courses would become. For many students, Farley said, the attraction of online convenience can be negated by the greater need for self-discipline. A hybrid

Central campus, decked out with banners to celebrate Washburn's 150 years.

model, containing some classroom work and some solely on computer, was working best.

"The fog is still surrounding us," he said, "regarding online programs."

New buildings, a new look

The Living Learning Center and the improvements to Moore Bowl and Whiting represented only the start of a campus facelift that continued well into the 2010s.

In 2004, a chapel originally constructed in 1996 on the grounds of the Menninger Foundation was moved to the Washburn campus through the fundraising efforts of alumni Carole Bloomfield Etzel and her husband, Tim Etzel. At Washburn the building was renamed Carole Chapel. It is used for meditation, for recitals and lectures by university groups, and by the public for weddings and other ceremonies.

In fall 2004 a Student Recreation and Wellness Center opened south of the football stadium. It featured a gym, exercise areas, running track and rock-climbing wall. That same year, a waterfall and rock garden marking the northeast corner of campus was dedicated at 17th Street and Washburn Avenue.

A 190-bed facility for upperclassmen further expanded campus living. An apartment-style structure in the southwest section of campus near KTWU, it was named Washburn Village when it opened in 2004. With its addition, the university could house 674 students on campus.

An art building southwest of the football stadium opened in summer 2005. Two years later, workers completed a 22,000-square-foot, two-story addition to and renovation of Stoffer Science Hall. It added one-third more space to the original, and was designed, through various measures, to use less energy.

In 2011, the Washburn regents approved a makeover of Morgan Hall to turn it into a campus entrance, welcome and student service center. Work began in early 2014. Also under construction was a $55 million crime

laboratory called a Forensic Science Center for the Kansas Bureau of Investigation and a new building for the Law School.

When stock markets and the housing market crashed in 2008, the endowments of American universities slipped, and so did Washburn's. From June 20 to December 15 of that year, the value of the endowment dropped from $124 million to $97 million. But the fund fought back and, after a record $16.5 million in donations in 2013, Washburn's endowment totaled $147 million, reaching $165 million in 2014. A national study found Washburn in the top 10 percent of public universities in return on its investment, and 30th among public schools in endowment per full-time-equivalent student. On July 1, 2010, the Washburn Endowment Association changed its name to the Washburn University Foundation.

Graduation Day 2014 in Lee Arena inside the Petro Allied Health Center.

As Washburn entered its 150th year, it looked forward to completing a $100 million fundraising campaign called 150 Forward, aiming to reach its goal by 2016. The campaign sought $35 million for student scholarships, $35 million for faculty and academic programs, $20 million for campus facilities and $10 million in annual giving.

Not for Ourselves Alone

Rice

Washburn

McVicar

Storrs Johnston

Most institutions don't survive a century and a half. In far less time, giant manufacturers have appeared, prospered and gone out of business. Banks have thrived and collapsed. Church congregations have formed and then dwindled and disappeared. Across America and certainly in Kansas, whole towns have started up and boomed and withered away. Colleges and schools that began with high hopes have passed from the scene, and mostly from memory.

Through 150 years, Washburn has endured and grown, its century-and-a-half journey a story of success. The path proved difficult at times, but Washburn and its community proved strong.

Washburn's founders held strong convictions about human rights, equality and the importance of education. In the 1860s, they dreamed of a college that would be a beacon for all, and also a leader in a growing community. Successive generations helped realize that dream.

Convictions, however, could not pay the bills. That required tireless efforts by administrators to build an institution worthy of support. Through the decades, friends near and far have given that support: Boswell, Crane, Garvey, Fink, Morgan, Mulvane, Mabee, Ritchie — and Ichabod Washburn. And there have been the people of Topeka, of Shawnee County and of all Kansas.

Through those 150 years, faculty members have dedicated their careers to creating and maintaining Washburn's reputation for high-quality education. Despite occasionally trying times of budget cuts, bouts with the administration and disagreements with students, many faculty have served Washburn for decades.

Topeka and Kansas have kept sending students, traditional or non-traditional, because Washburn has always been a good place for the community to learn.

"We are a teaching institution," Farley said. "I tell the deans that's the most important job we have: hiring good teachers, teachers who accept this as what we are."

"That's our history. That's our legacy: We've been a university of opportunity since we opened."

— President Jerry Farley

Small class sizes are important, too; less than 2 percent of the university's classes contain more than 50 students, and Farley estimates the student-faculty ratio at 15 to one. The small class size not only draws new students, but also attracts transfers from the big state universities: students who feel lost amid tens of thousands of other students.

Additionally, Washburn has an "open-admission" policy that allows even underachieving high school graduates to enter if they meet certain requirements in university coursework.

"That's our history," Farley says, "that's our legacy: We've been a university of opportunity since we opened."

Graduates have gone out in the world and done well, and many have remembered Washburn with their moral and financial support. In turn, the endowment has helped students meet the sometimes daunting costs of higher

Leavitt

Womer

Scott

Dole

Menninger

education through scholarships.

Enduring for 150 years requires perseverance, and the leaders, faculty and students of Washburn have demonstrated that in abundance. It also requires adaptability and resilience. Those have been marks of Washburn from the earliest days, when the newborn state of Kansas could scarcely bring forward students who were ready for college. Through its Academy, Washburn undertook to prepare them.

Perseverance, resilience and adaptability also characterized Washburn through two World Wars and the Great Depression. Those traits resounded in the late 1930s and early 1940s, when the community voted a resounding "Yes" to keeping the institution alive. And they proved indispensable after the tornado of 1966 tore up the buildings but not the heart of the university.

No institution survives waves of good times and bad for 150 years without energetic leaders, able faculty and staff and a dedicated army of well-wishers. In good times, Washburn leaders expanded the campus and improved academic programs. In bad times, they kept up the fight to keep Washburn alive.

Many of the young people who prepared for lives and careers at Washburn became loyal and often vocal alumni. As they grew older, generations of them gave back to the school that gave them an education.

The small band of believers who in the 1860s brought the institution into being thought that the citizenry ought to have the benefits of higher eduction. The result, they were convinced, would create a prosperous city for those around them and for generations to follow. Their community, the founders believed, would be served well by skilled and thoughtful members and leaders. Fittingly, early in the 20th century one professor bestowed this motto on Washburn: *Non Nobis Solum*, "Not for Ourselves Alone."

The story of Washburn is one of great changes, of sometimes difficult times and of a common thread: an institution open to all who want to learn and to take their place building and leading the community around them.

Through its people, Washburn has built the foundation that has stood firm for 150 years and prepared it for the next 150.

Fletcher

Garvey

Farley

Acknowledgments, sources and image credits

The journey through Washburn's rich history takes a researcher straight into the heart of Mabee Library, where the University Archives contain a treasury of information. Archivist Martha Imparato knows volumes about the ins and outs, the twists and turns of the university's 150-year life. If there's a question she cannot answer, she'll pursue it doggedly until she can. She provided tremendous help with the research for this book and excellent guidance and criticism along the way.

Other Washburn veterans — former faculty, former students and friends of the institution — helped with their own memories and insights. Among them were Bill Wagnon, Carol Vogel, Robert Richmond and Reed Whittaker. Members of the Washburn 150 Committee who read the manuscript gave useful advice on content and style.

Sources

The vast majority of the sources listed here are from the University Archives. Record groups are indicated by WUA.

Records of the President's Office - General Office Files are abbreviated RPO-GOF.

Copies of most of the articles, whether from Washburn's own periodicals or from historical quarterlies or magazines, are also filed in the University Archives.

Chapter One: Creating a College

The Kansas Historical Quarterly published a thorough, two-part history of Washburn's earliest days by Russell K. Hickman, "Lincoln College, Forerunner of Washburn Municipal University" in its February 1950 issue. Hickman included extensive information about the founders of Lincoln College in a two-part series, "Lewis Bodwell, Frontier Preacher" published in *The Kansas Historical Quarterly* in August and November 1943.

Much information came from Lincoln College documents at WUA; from printed "Reminiscences" by Harvey Rice; from a manuscript by Paul Adams, "John Ritchie: 1817-1887," and from two articles in the November 1991 issue of *The Shawnee County Historical Society Bulletin*, "John Ritchie in the Context of History" by Bill Cecil-Fronsman and "John Ritchie: Portrait of an Uncommon Man" by Mary Ritchie Jarboe.

In 1934, Washburn's *Kaw* yearbook printed a manuscript by Harvey Rice entitled "Birth on the Prairies."

The nature and background of the denomination that encompassed Washburn's founders, nationally and in Kansas, is described in these books and website: Charles M. Correll, *A Century of Congregationalism in Kansas 1854-1954*. Topeka: The Kansas Congregational and Christian Conference, 1953; J. William T. Youngs, *The Congregationalists*. New York: Greenwood Publishing Group, 1998, and "Congregationalism" on the website of United Church of Christ, **www.ucc.org**.

Also:

Richard Cordley's article about Lincoln College in *The Kansas Telephone*, July 1890.

Topeka at 150: Celebrating the Sesquicentennial of the Capital City of Kansas, published by *The Topeka Capital-Journal*, 2004.

The *Ichabodian* yearbook, 1915, renamed from *Kaw* to mark the 50th anniversary of the college.

Chapter Two: Building a Foundation

WUA original handwritten records show the financial struggle faced by the trustees: Minutes, Lincoln College Board of Trustees, 1867; Washburn College Board of Trustees, 1870, 1871 and 1873, all in the First Secretary's Book at WUA. Also, these folders in WUA Lincoln College Records: Lewis Bodwell Papers, Original Treasurer's Book, 1865-1869, Subscription Book, 1865-1869 and Miscellaneous Correspondence.

Also:

"The First President of Washburn College," *The Weekly Review*, Nov. 18, 1897.

Thomas S. Harding, "Washburn's 'Forgotten Presidents,' Horatio Q. Butterfield." *Washburn Alumni*, spring 1979.

John Daniel Bright, "The Generous Ichabod." *The Shawnee County Historical Society Bulletin*, March 1951.

WUA RPO - GOF, Peter McVicar, with these folders: Fundraising, 1875-1885; Development Plans; Construction of Main Building; Preparatory School, and Treasurer's Reports, FY 1891-93. Included is an essay about McVicar, D.L. McEachron's "Peter McVicar: The 'Grand Old Man' of Washburn College," published in *The Washburn College Bulletin* of October 1933. Several manuscripts were written by McVicar containing important information used in this chapter: "A Report on Washburn College" delivered to the Kansas Congregationalists' General Association in 1873; "An Historical Sketch of Washburn College" read at the dedication of Boswell Hall, October 23, 1886; a McVicar article dated February 4, 1887; McVicar's speech on the 25th anniversary of the college in 1890, as quoted in *The Shawnee County Historical Bulletin* of March 1951, and "Story of the College," a paper read to the General Association in October 1892. It also includes the agreement between the trustees and the College Society dated October 6, 1873.

The files also hold reminiscences about McVicar prepared by former students and faculty in the early 1930s.

WUA RPO - GOF, Annual Reports, 1893-1961, contains McVicar's report for academic year 1893-1894. McVicar's note on "Cost of Building and Improvements" thru June 1877 tells some of the story of the building that became Rice Hall. More is contained in "Story of Rice Hall," *The Washburn Review*, Jan. 28,1914.

Also used:

S. H. Fairfield "Many Discouragements in Early Days of Washburn," article dated 1914.

Hermione Van Laer Adams, " College Hill, Past and Present," *The Shawnee County Historical Society Bulletin*, December 1962.

Washburn College Catalog, 1878-1879 and 1884-1885.

The Washburn Review.

Washburn College Bulletin, various articles copied for WUA's Clippings file.

Kaw yearbook, 1909 and 1934.

Ichabodian yearbook, 1915.

The Helianthus yearbook, 1897.

Former librarian Thomas Harding wrote a series of articles, "Washburn's Forgotten Presidents – II: George M. Herrick: The Quiet President" in *Washburn Alumni*. Also helpful on Herrick were issues of *The Topeka Daily Capital*, particularly in 1899 and 1901. In Herrick's own words is "President Herrick's Farewell," *The Washburn Review*, Volume 18, Number 2.

The WUA clippings file has an article, "Humble Little Institution Up the River," from *Washburn Alumnus*, September 1967, with of early history of the college.

Also used:

Russell Hickman's articles in *The Kansas Historical Quarterly* (See above).

Various articles from *The Topeka Daily Capital* and *The Topeka State Journal*.

James F. Zimmerman, "The Washburn Story," unpublished history of the institution prepared for the 1965 centennial celebration.

Faculty member J.T. Lovewell's account of his arrival in Topeka, originally published in *The Washburn Review*, January 3, 1917, and reprinted in Zimmerman's "Washburn Story."

"The Day the President Came to Washburn," *Washburn Alumni*, October/November 1992.

Chapter Three: New Momentum

WUA RPO - GOF, Norman Plass, folders include Card Playing and Dancing, which contains Carrie Nation's 1901 letter from a Topeka jail. Other folders: Fundraising and Washburn College History; Speeches, 1902-1908; Land Sale Agreement, 1907, and Medical College, 1903.

Also used:

Norman Plass, "Seven Years' Report," June 21, 1908.

WUA RPO - GOF, 1893-1961, Sanders' report for academic year 1908-190.

The Washburn Review, 1901, No. 9.

Washburn College Bulletin, various articles copied in WUA's Clippings file, including March 1903 on campus buildings.

Washburn Campus & Field, various articles.

D.M. Fisk, "The Story of a Year's Expansion," article evidently issued for commencement in 1903.

D.L. McEachron, "Period of Expansion, 1896-1905." Paper read at 40th anniversary of Washburn's founding and printed in the *Kaw*, 1906.

Kaw, 1904, 1905, 1907, 1907.

Thomas Harding, "Washburn's Forgotten Presidents – III: Norman Plass: Educational Entrepreneur." *Washburn Alumni*, fall 1979.

"Two Cornerstones Recently Uncovered" and "Secret Cornerstone Explained in Letter," *The Washburn Review*, October 22, 1966.

Harold C. Evans, "College Football in Kansas." *The Kansas Historical Quarterly*, August 1940.

WUA RPO - GOF, Frank Sanders. Folders include Financial Reports, ca 1908-1913; Faculty and Staff, 1909-1912; Faculty Meeting Minutes; Campus, ca 1909-1911; Conference of the Colleges of the Middle West,1911; Kansas Congregationalist Conference, 1911; Law School, 1910-1912; Medical College, 1909-1911; Recruitment of Students, 1906-1911; Student Housing and Board, ca 1909; Summer School, 1910-1911; Trustees, Board of, ca 1908-1913; Trustees, Board of, Executive Committee, ca 1908-1911, and Miscellaneous Correspondence.

Also:

"Big College Pageant Held at Washburn," *The Topeka State Journal*, June 9, 1915.

WUA RPO - GOF, Parley Womer, folders Personal correspondence, 1898-1935, and World War I.

WUA RPO - GOF, 1893-1961, Womer's reports for academic years ending 1917, 1918 and 1919.

WUA RPO - GOF, Phillip King, in folder Fraternities and Sororities an unsigned address at Freshman Convocation, Sept. 20, 1937, in which the old bell's history is covered.

Martha Imparato, "Greek Social Societies at Washburn," *Washburn Alumni*, Summer 2004.

"President Frank Knight Sanders" and "Dr. Sanders Re-elected." *The Washburn Review*, June 1913.

Thomas Harding, "Washburn's Forgotten Presidents IV [Frank Sanders]" *Washburn Alumni*, winter 1980.

Chapter Four: Modern Times to Hard Times

WUA RPO - GOF, Womer, folders include Law School, 1918-1931; Kirkpatrick, J.E.; Investigation by AAUP, ca 1917-1923; American Citizenship Department, 1925-1929.

WUA RPO - GOF, King, folders include Enrollment data, 1914-1940; General Education Board, 1923-1927; American Citizenship Program; College-Church relations, ca 1931-1941; Fundraising, ca 1930-1941; Seventy-Fifth Anniversary; Admissions office; Student housing, ca 1933-1941; Report of the Dean of Women, 1935; Student Personnel Services, ca 1937-1940; Complaints; Miscellaneous Correspondence, 1932-1941; Engineering Department, 1938; Alumni and former students; Insurance, ca 1932-1939; Law school, ca 1938-1941; Faculty, ca 1935-1941; Faculty Rules and By-laws, ca 1937-

1939; Board of Trustees, 1937-1941; Faculty and Staff Correspondence; American Citizenship Department, 1925-1941; Fraternities; Allen Fellowship and Loan Fund, ca 1934-1941; Commencement; Treasurer's Report, 1940-1942; Athletics, 1930-1941, and Alumni and Former Students.

Also:

Letter from President King to E. G. Buckland, October 17, 1938.

Board of Trustees Minutes, 1890-1941, at the Washburn University Foundation.

WUA RPO - GOF, Green, folder Alumni Association.

WUA Records of the President's Office – Annual Reports, 1893-1961, King's report for academic year ending in 1940.

Frazer & Torbert, accountants, "Washburn College Survey, May 1940." Washburn University Foundation.

WUA Records of the President's Office – Annual Reports, 1893-1961, King's report for academic year ending 1941.

Letter, Women to Trustees, June 3, 1929, at Washburn University Foundation.

The Washburn Review, particulary October 20, 1920; September 1, 1928; October 25, 1935, and April 4, 1941.

Washburn College Bulletin,October 1, 1930, "Administration in Hands of Mr. King for a Few Months," And December 1940, "Alumni committee Believes Municipalization Best Plan."

WUA Records of Boards, Committees and Councils, Student Council 1922-1939

WUA Records of the Vice President for Financial Affairs and Treasurer. File includes "Treasurer's Report for the Fiscal Year July 1, 1940 to June 30, 1941."

WUA Clipping files, Law School.

Interview with Bill Wagnon.

The Topeka Daily Capital, particularly August 30, 1959.

Kaw 1919, 1922, 1938.

James F. Zimmerman, "The Washburn Story," unpublished manuscript (see notes in earlier chapters)..

Chapter Five: The Municipal Way

WUA RPO - GOF, King, folder Municipal University status, 1940-1941.

WUA RPO - GOF, Stoffer, folders Speeches, 1942-1961, and Miscellaneous Documents.

WUA RPO - GOF, Sponberg, folders Personal File; Budget Matters, 1962-1963; Inauguration, 1962, and Resignation, 1965.

WUA RPO - GOf, Henderson, folders Inauguration, 1965; Report of an Accreditation Visit, 1965, and General Study of Washburn University, 1964.

WUA Records of the Vice President for Finance, 1932-1959, "Treasurer's report for the fiscal year July 1, 1940 to June 30, 1941."

Kaw, particularly 1942 and 1956.

Washburn University Timeline online at Washburn website, **www.washburn.edu**.

James F. Zimmerman, "The Washburn Story," unpublished manuscript (see notes in earlier chapters).

Report of the President to the Board of Trustees.

Washburn University Bulletin, particularly February 1946 and December 1952.

David Marannis, "Exploring How Dole Thinks," *The Washington Post*, August 4, 1996

Robert Clark, "Washburn University Looks to Glowing Future," *The Kansas City Star*, October 3, 1962.

Chapter Six: Down, But Not Out

Jerry Dean Kendall, "Aftermath of a Tornado," Ed. D. dissertation, Indiana University, June 1970.

The Topeka Capital-Journal, June 9, 1966.

WUA President's Annual Reports, 1965-1966, 1970-1971 through 1975-1976, 1982-1983 through 1985-1986, 1988-1989, 1990-1991,1993-1994 and 1995-1996.

Bonar Menninger, *And Hell Followed With It: Life and Death in a Kansas Tornado*. 2011

Washburn Alumni

WUA RPO- GOF, Henderson, folder Tornado; Washburn College Bible, and Board of Regents and Last Year, 1980.

WUA RPO - GOF, Green, folder Five-year Strategic Plan and Board of Regents, Miscellaneous.

WUA Records of the President's Office – General Office Files, Stoffer, folder Written Statements, 1953-1960.

WUA RPO - GOF, Duggan, folder Memorial Service.

WUA RPO - GOF, Thompson, folders Minutes, Senior Staff Meeting, March 8, 1996, and General Faculty Meeting, 1995.

Kaw, various years and particularly 1996

Chapter Seven: 150 and Going Strong

Interview with Jerry Farley, June 2014.

Interview with Bill Wagnon, June 2014.

WUA President's annual reports, 1998-1999 and 1999-2005.

The Topeka Capital-Journal, multiple issues and articles, 1997-2014, available at **cjonline.com**.

The Washburn Review, particularly February 17, 2002; May 5, 2004; April 6, 2009; February 17, 2010; April 13, 2011; September 26, 2011; October 30, 2013;

WUA Clippings Files, particularly Whiting Field House, Washburn Endowment Association,

Washburn Alumni, fall 2006, winter 2006, spring 2007, summer 2007, fall 2007

Image credits

All images are from the Washburn University Archives, except these:

Page 2, 6, 158, 159, 160, 163, 164, 165, 167, 168, 169, 170-171: Peggy Clark, Washburn University Photographer

Page 7: Courtesy Bob Dole.

Page 8, 17: Library of Congress, Geography and Map Division

Page 19, 21: Library of Congress, Prints and Photographs Division

Page 13, 14-15, 22-23, 36 (upper left): Kansas Historical Society

Index